The Greatest Gift

The Greatest Gift

John Davis

With best wishes

John Davis

ISBN 978-0-9573353-0-1
Printed and bound by Good News, Ongar, England
Published by John Davis Publications
4 Streche Road, Swanage, Dorset, BH19 1NF

FOREWORD

By the Rt Revd Peter Nott
(Bishop of Norwich 1985-1991)

This book will speak powerfully to many seekers after truth and meaning, because it is written by someone who has been immersed in the world of science and technology, but whose vision goes beyond the assumed conflicts between that world and religion, to describe deep insights into the vital connections between the material and spiritual.

John Davis writes simply, clearly and profoundly of the central truths of Christianity. He helpfully shares his personal journey of faith, with an honesty that does not avoid hard questions.

When he saw the first draft of the book some years ago, the late Bishop Stephen Verney wrote that he found it 'very fresh, and whole and moving; free from all theological jargon, which draws out the great truths, expressing them in layman's language.' I entirely endorse that judgment, from a man who was one of the foremost communicators of the faith in modern times. John Davis has written a book which is itself a great gift to a wide variety of readers.

Peter Nott
March 2010

INTRODUCTION

Shortly after Winston Churchill became Prime Minister in World War II, he told the nation that we were involved in a struggle to preserve Christian civilisation from the barbarism of fascism. In 1940 most people in Britain understood what he meant by Christian civilization because they had learned about Jesus Christ and Christianity. They were very familiar with the meaning of the celebrations of Christmas, Lent, Easter and Whitsuntide.

Sadly, seventy years later, when a Prime Minister speaks about the need to recover Christian values, many people do not have a clear idea of what he is talking about. Unlike previous generations, they have not been taught about the true meaning of Christianity. Consequently, all kinds of ideas and beliefs are filling the vacuum; with the worship of money being most common. We are living as though increasing monetary wealth is the only way to solve life's problems and increase happiness. Now it is beginning to threaten the existence of our life on earth. So, although fascism was defeated, it appears that Christian civilisation in Britain was not secured; its values having been eroded by the indiscriminate growth of monetary values. If the threat to life is to be defeated, this time the struggle is for the hearts and minds and wills of people here at home.

One of the wisest men of the 20th century was Dr E F Schumacher. He began as an atheist and became a Christian. He is world famous for his book Small Is Beautiful. In it, he dealt with the challenge we face. In the final page, he remarks that the guidance we need is, 'not in science or technology, the value of which depends on the ends they serve, but is still to be found in the traditional wisdom of mankind'. For him, and the British people, it is in traditional Christianity, which is found essentially in the person of Jesus Christ and in his teaching, his claims, his bequests and his legacy.

It is a most extraordinary thing that fourteen hundred years after Christianity was first introduced to Britain, by Saint Augustine in the south and Saint Aidan in the north, that so many of the present population know so little about Jesus, its founder, when almost all that is civilised and that we value in these islands originates from him.

It is not the intention of this book to attempt to retell the story of Jesus, because the four gospels cannot be bettered. For some of the millions of people who have had the misfortune of not hearing 'The Greatest Story Ever Told', it is the intention of this book to provide some light from Christian experience on such questions as, 'What is the essence of Christianity?' and, 'Does it make a difference to the way a person lives now?' as well as, 'If so, what difference does it make?'

All over the world, hundreds of millions of people, today and over the last two thousand years would confirm that complete trust in Jesus is such a great gift that it is the most rewarding one in anyone's life. It is even worth dying for because, through it, we are able to enjoy life with God.

CONTENTS

Foreword   v

Introduction   vii

Chapter 1   The Context   1

Chapter 2   Christianity – Actually, what is it?   11

Chapter 3   The Historic Jesus   19

Chapter 4   The Contemporary Jesus   39

Chapter 5   What is it that only Jesus can give us?   51

Chapter 6   Consequences   59

Chapter 7   Beliefs – Christianity and Churchianity   79

Chapter One

The Context

Let us start from where we are in 2010. The 21st century world is very different from the world of my childhood. In the 20's and 30's, despite all the economic and social problems of the period, there was an underlying feeling of continuity and stability. Although there were fewer church-goers than in previous decades, and a few free thinkers on the fringe, there was a feeling of almost universal acceptance within Britain of shared Christian values. Any suggestion that we were not a Christian country would have been hotly contested by most people. In retrospect, the feeling was, to a certain extent, false. The continuity for some time had been broken – maybe from the time of the Enlightenment – and the stability had been shattered by World War I. Nevertheless, those feelings of continuity and stability were real to most people. The promise of onward and upward progress – shades of H G Wells – informed by science and realised through technology, was rarely questioned by ordinary people. From a narrowly British point of view, the Empire looked good for a long time to come. There did not seem to be too much to worry about from Ghandi or other minor irritants.

How different things feel over fifty years later to the present generation of children. To many, science and technology pose more of a threat than a promise of progress. Britain is not even among the winners in the language of international winners and losers, let alone the major Imperial power. There are few remains of a pretence that we are a Christian country; indeed, it is proudly declared that we are a multi-faith society, which, in practical terms, means that there is no shared faith. As all pervasive is the idea that we are a multi-cultural society, which is practical terms to a young person means that there is no single set of shared values or principles as guidelines for everyone to live by. In this sense, they are much more confused and much less well off than young people in a primitive tribe. All sense of stability, structure and order have all but gone. Everything is equal and up for grabs. Individualism is all that remains. Pop music, videos and drugs tell complementary stories – a retreat from the frightening, meaningless and purposeless world around them into a world of total fantasy.

How could such a dramatic change have come about? Or is it that these are just as much illusions as were the feelings of continuity and stability that existed between the war years?

Where did the old continuity and stability come from and what has happened which has caused us to lose them? In my engineering work, as, indeed, in all other aspects of life, continuity depends on the orderliness of the natural world. Unless I can be sure that the laws of thermodynamics will continue to operate in the future as they have in the past, I am completely unable to design or build any kind of useful engine. But it is not only in matters of material behaviour that I need to be orderly if my work is to be done for any purpose; I must also be reasonably confident that if I go on producing washing machines, all the people who use them will not suddenly change their habits and cease washing their clothes. For life to be able to continue, there has to be orderliness in the way that both materials and human beings behave. If there is to be continuity, life requires both a set of principles, or laws, that are applicable to material objects, and another set of principles that govern the behaviour of human beings and other living things.

There are some important differences in the ways that the two sets of principles operate. The laws of physics are remorseless. Any brazen attempt to overthrow them, to contravene them, results in immediate and unwelcome results. If you put a ten pound note in a flame, that note, and no other, will immediately burn. If, however, you choose to ignore the principles governing human behaviour, there will just as certainly be adverse consequences, which may not be felt immediately, and may often not harm the perpetrator but produce other undesirable effects. Both sets of principles control the earth and life on the earth; they are the basis of continuity. They are natural laws that are built into the fabric of existence. They apply to everything and to all people everywhere and in all ages. Unlike manmade laws, they cannot be modified or repealed. There are, of course, other laws that are manmade which do change from time to time and differ from place to place. Whatever they are, however, they cannot influence the operation of natural laws, but it is quite possible for manmade laws that are not in harmony with them to be unintentionally introduced.

If that happens, harmful consequences will be as inevitable as if there was a deliberate intention to contravene natural law. It is possible that attempts to sweep away in recent years some of what appeared to be pointless, arbitrary and illiberal traditional taboos may now be showing signs of having contravened principles that are part of the nature of things. There are certain things that nature will not tolerate which may well appear to us to be an unwelcome restriction of our freedom. The notion that we are totally free beings able to follow our own personal inclinations is nonsense. To some people, that is what 'doing your own

3

thing' suggests. The value of historical experience is that it can give us some ideas of where the limits to our freedom exist. It is striking that the limits to our freedom and the nature of natural law governing human behaviour have been known and formulated in various ways for many centuries. It is somewhat surprising that they have existed for much longer than the formulation of most physical laws.

How an understanding of natural law came about is an important question. Fortunately, the discovery of the physical laws is recent enough for us to have some idea of how their delivery occurred. The discoverers – men like Sir Isaac Newton – were actively seeking to understand the ways in which things behaved in an orderly manner. But it seems that there was usually more to the discovery than an inescapable conclusion derived from observations.

For example, Sir William Bragg, who followed Lord Rutherford as Professor of Physics at the Cavendish Laboratory in Cambridge, used the following words in a lecture:

'When one has long sought for a clue to the secret of nature, and is rewarded by grasping some part of the answer, it comes as a blinding flash of revelation. It comes as something new, more simple and more aesthetically satisfying than anything one could have created in one's own mind. The conviction is of something revealed and not something imagined.'

Perhaps if more people knew that the marvellous discoveries of scientists, like Bragg and Einstein, were the result of revelation, and not only human intellect, they would not be quite so dismissive of the traditional conviction that the natural laws of human behaviour, formulated by people like Moses, were also the result of a personal experience of revelation.

So it is no exaggeration to say that the feeling of continuity that has been a common experience in Britain over many centuries was founded on a conviction that there are remorseless principles that govern human behaviour, and that knowledge and understanding of these laws came through a blinding flash of revelation to an individual person and were not just the product of a human fallible mind.

What, then, about the feeling of stability? Again, as an engineer, I have to be careful not to get into technical deep water, for stability is an important engineering topic. There is stability of aircraft and other vehicles in motion, stability of structural members under stress and stability of complete structures such as buildings or bridges. For complete structures, there are three essential things required for stability – a sound foundation, members that are strong enough and fixings that are capable of holding things together come what may. If any single one of these three things is missing, the structure will be unstable.

Societies also require all of several elements to exist if they are to be stable and, similarly, if any of these things is missing, the society can become unstable and will almost certainly feel so. Like the fixings in an engineering structure, there is one essential element that plays a vital part in holding everything together. It is a kind of social glue that has a binding effect. The nature of this glue can vary. It may be a common set of ideas such as are shared within an ideological political movement; it may be a body of dogma such as exists in some religions, or it may be love for and allegiance to a person, such as exists as the primary focus of the Christian religion and which differentiates it from the other main religions.

5

So far as Britain is concerned, for almost two thousand years it has not been a body of ideas or a dogma that has been the cement in our society. Until comparatively recently, it has been a widespread acceptance of the person of Jesus Christ and all that he represents, who is believed to be the Incarnate Son of God Almighty; not merely a good and great man, nor a profound teacher, though he was these things as well.

Gradually, this binding factor in British life has been eroded and no other social glue has taken its place. The vacuum that has been left has resulted in a state of chaos of conflicting ideas and values that has undermined confidence and morale. People do not know what they are part of, nor what it is that they can look up to. In place of a shared devotion and allegiance, we now have divisiveness and individualism.

The old continuity and stability that was felt in Britain for so many centuries lasted as long as there was a common acceptance of the principles that are part of the natural order of things which govern human behaviour and a widespread devotion to the person of Jesus Christ, the only Son of God, and all that he represented to the common people. This was the basis of traditional British life that gave citizens a sense of belonging and common identity.

Doubtless, there are many causes for this loss of conviction and of devotion and allegiance to Jesus Christ and the Christian faith as well as a loss of willingness to accept and submit to traditional patterns of human behaviour.

Some years ago, I was involved in an enquiry to find out what helped or hindered practising Christians in the living out of their faith in working life. One thing that was clear was that many of those involved in the study, myself included, had absorbed a partial and watered down version of what Jesus Christ represented and what a full expression of the Gospel means.

For example, whereas there has been much stress on the compassionate side of Jesus, not so much attention had been paid to the tough, judgemental aspects of his life or his insistence on the observance of Judaic law informed by love. Much had been made of the need to observe the commandment to love one's neighbour, but little had been given to the teaching that distinguishes the teaching of Jesus from the traditional historic rabbinical teaching which was his call to love one's enemies. There had been great emphasis on the redemptive work of God, but very little about the creative work. There seemed to have been a nervousness about creation, as though it was entirely the preserve of science and not religion.

A widespread distortion in teaching was the emphasis on the individual and the neglect of social justice which is one of the main themes of both Judaism and Christianity. There seemed to have been a polarisation.

On the one hand, teaching of the faith had retreated into what some describe as pietistic, another worldly perception of the faith. On the other, the supernatural aspects had been progressively diluted until what remained was barely distinguishable from scientific humanism. The latter lacked the binding power of the traditional Christian faith, whilst the former, which had an appeal for a minority of people with strong religious inclinations, seemed to have little attraction to the mass of ordinary people.

As a consequence of these trends and other causes, the Christian faith has become a minority influence in modern Britain, despite the fact that the great majority of people declare a belief in God and there is a hunger, and a search – especially amongst the young – for some form of spiritual satisfaction.

The Christian faith is by no means in decline around the world. Indeed, in many parts, its influence is growing strong. Sometimes it is replacing primitive religions; elsewhere, it gains strength in traditional Christian countries when the Church is persecuted. Some years ago, it was reported that a Chinese leader had said that the one spirit they had failed to suppress was the Christian Holy Spirit. The problem of decline in Britain is not a consequence of any shortcoming in the faith itself, rather, it seems to be associated with inadequate evangelism and a failure of leadership that gives an impression of a lack of conviction regarding basic principles in human affairs and an unwillingness to make a firm stand.

When she was in England, Mother Theresa was asked to compare London and Calcutta. She spoke of the destitution in Calcutta and added, 'But you have a worse poverty here, there is a loneliness and a poverty of the spirit.'

A priority for the present is to recover a full perception and a lively understanding of the Christian faith that, for so long, provided a firm foundation and a binding force for the people of Britain. If as individuals, we can recapture a new vision of Jesus Christ and all that he represents, not only shall we find personal spiritual satisfaction and meaning for our own lives, but a new spirit will begin to appear in society as order replaces chaos, as a sense of interdependence and community takes the place of individualism and as suspicion and distrust give way to co-operation and caring. It will be a new vision that will demand a personal response and commitment and its consequences will depend upon the extent to which we, individually and corporately, allow the spirit of God to work through us.

This book can do no more than help some of those people who find a clear understanding and full perception of the Christian faith difficult to obtain through conventional literature or through such learning opportunities as Churches are able to provide. Most readers will have some notion of what Christianity is. A poll would show that there are many different pictures in the minds of individual readers, therefore, we need to start our journey of discovery by clearing the undergrowth, removing any mistaken ideas and making space for those that are helpful to flourish.

Once we are quite clear about what Christianity actually is, we then must encounter Jesus, the historic Jesus, on whom the faith rests. He was a Jew and, although, at times, he was very critical of some of his contemporary religious leaders, there is no doubt that he was devoted to the Jewish scriptures and law. Indeed, he is reported as having said that he did not come to destroy them but to fulfil them.

If we are to understand and commit ourselves to the person of Jesus Christ, we must come to terms with the teaching embodied in the Old Testament as well as the New Testament. So the chapter that deals with the historic Jesus is followed by several that consider some aspects of the faith that he adhered to and which seem, to me, to be particularly important in the modern world.

Chapter Two

Christianity – Actually, what is it?

At the beginning of his book, *A Guide For The Perplexed*, E F Schumacher wrote about a visit that he made to Leningrad. When he enquired why his street map showed only some of the churches that he could see around him, an interpreter told him that the ones that were still used as living churches were not shown because religion was not part of Communist reality.

Communism is not alone in denying the existence of some aspects of human experience as part of reality. It is an increasing feature of the spread of materialism in all parts of the developed world that has sought to separate some things and give them either unique or special significance. For example, economics pays particular attention to those parts of economic relations that involve monetary transactions. It is little interested in other forms of wealth - creation and distribution, like home cooking or voluntary social services.

Science confines itself to those common things that occur in a regular fashion, ones which can be observed and measured. Other things that do not fit into a contemporary scientific world are set on one side. For the time being, they are treated as inexplicable oddities which may at some future date be explained in the light of new scientific knowledge.

In engineering, we are not free from this tendency. In power stations, and in other forms of power generation, we are so preoccupied with efficiency and reliability from the operator's point of view that we overlook other problems we might be creating, like acid rain. When we work out the cost of producing a unit of electricity, we leave out the cost of the damage that acid rain causes.

The most important of such divisions has been the habit of considering the world of material things and the world of the spirit as separate. It is a very primitive notion. However, it is completely alien to a Christian view of the world, because a central point of the Christian faith is that God, The Almighty Creator, who is Spirit, is identified with his creation by entering it through the person of Jesus Christ. That conviction is so central that its reality is manifested at every celebration of the Holy Communion when spiritual gifts are received through the medium of bread and wine. Christianity does not belong to some exclusive spiritual life that is separate from our material existence. Neither is it only to do with people. For God so loved the world that he gave his only begotten Son... There is no a hair on our head not a grain of sand that is outside the embrace of God's love.

It has truly been said that Christianity is the most materialistic of all religions. In life on earth, material and spiritual are as inseparable as the two sides of a coin. It is common experience that material processes can be influenced by the mind and the will. There is untold evidence that spiritual forces can, likewise, manifest themselves.

People can be excused for thinking that Christianity is an exclusive religion if the impression given by the Churches is the touchstone. But there are so many stories told about Jesus that make it absolutely clear that there was nobody that he would exclude from friendship, and he was much criticised for consorting with people of ill repute.

In his letter to the Galatians, Paul summed it up by saying, 'There is no such thing as Jew or Greek, slave or freeman, male or female. All are one in Christ Jesus.' There are no boundaries of nationality, creed, rank or sex in Christianity. It is all inclusive and universal.

One of the most common perceptions equates Christianity with a moral code. People say that behaviour is not Christian. In his life on earth, Jesus set an unparalleled example of human behaviour that went far beyond mere sinlessness, according to Jewish moral code; but he did not formulate a new and superior moral code to replace Mosaic law.

There was a question asked of a radio panel which enquired whether morality could be taught without any religious context. All agreed that it could be. To my surprise, all said that they considered it was easier to teach as part of a religion. It seems to me that it is more difficult to teach that way, and if the religion is rejected, it's likely that the morality will be also. Although three of the four panellists professed to be Christians, none said that the important Christian element in morality is that we are left alone to live our lives as best we can. We are offered the gift of the Holy Spirit to guide and help us if we seek such aid. That applies to everyone and not only to people who call themselves Christians. God is not deaf to anyone's cry for help. Jesus has given us the target to aim at through the example of his life on earth, and we are called upon to follow him. And he has not left us helpless, but has given us the gift of the indwelling Holy Spirit to sustain us.

Another misconception of Christianity is that it is a philosophy of life based on a set of fundamental assumptions and doctrinal belief. No doubt, philosophies of life can be developed from any particular formulation of a Christian creed, and many thinking Christian people work out a philosophy of life for themselves that is consistent with their

13

basic beliefs. But that does not mean that Christianity is to be considered as a particular philosophy of life. Certainly, Christians hold certain beliefs in common, but it is not the holding of these beliefs which, of itself, makes them Christians, even though assent to a particular creed is part of initiation into the institutional Church.

Christianity is like marriage. It is a relationship between men, women and God, freely entered into by each person at God's invitation. Like Holy Matrimony, it is an unconditional commitment for life to the living Christ. It is entered into through an act of self giving in response to the sacrificial self giving of God in the life, death and resurrection of Jesus. Like a marriage, it has to be worked at if it is to deepen and flourish. For a Christian, it means getting to know God's mind and will better day by day so that every action may be pleasing to the one that is loved. Because there is no corner of life that is outside of God's concern, all life's activities are involved in this getting to know. Of necessity, this relationship becomes increasingly the dominant one in the life of a Christian. Because it is a living relationship, communication is two way. There is an initiative and response from both God and people.

But Holy Matrimony is only 'until death us do part'. The relationship between God and his people is an everlasting one that is not limited to our material existence. There is no contradiction with the point made earlier that Christianity does not belong to some spiritual life that is separate from the material world. The life of the spirit can and does exist independently, and it is the ultimate reality of life, not subject to the processes of material decay. But within the material world, spirit and matter are interdependent.

There is another important comparison to be made with marriage.

The relationship between man and wife is not just a one to one affair. It is a social relationship. Of course, this is why, even in a secular ceremony, it is a public affair. A new family is formed which is part of the wider family of the community. In the same way the relationship that is formed between God and an individual is an inseparable part of the wider family of God. It is the whole community of those who have committed themselves to Jesus Christ that is 'The Bride of Christ'. No-one can be a lone Christian.

That is why there is a public ceremony of the sacrament of baptism. It is not only a matter of welcoming a newcomer into the Church – the family of God – it is more mysteriously celebrating publicly the commitment of the new life relationship between the person and God and the Family of God. Whatever form baptism may take, there is, in the ritual, an expression of abandoning an old life and entering into a new and different one in a community.

Perhaps this is the true meaning of conversion – the desire and the intention of abandoning a self-centred life for a life of sacrificial love for Christ and the whole of creation within a community that is similarly committed. Because of the personal relationship nature of Christian life there can be no absolute obligation to subscribe to a particular dogma or code of behaviour. The only conditions are honesty and sincerity of intention and faith in the love that binds. The door of entry is wide open to all. God's love knows no bounds.

'Nothing in my hands I bring' are words of a famous hymn, and that is the only dowry we have to offer. Because of this, and because of the social nature of Christian initiation, it is not surprising that, in the early days of the Church, whole families were baptised at the same time.

15

Of course, this is not to say that what we believe or do not believe is unimportant. It only means that we are not banned from the family of God on that account.

A marriage between two people can give meaning and purpose to otherwise unfulfilling lives. Commitment to Christ always gives ultimate purpose and meaning to a person's life. But this benefit is merely a by-product which we may hope to gain. It cannot be our aim any more than it can be the aim of a marriage. Such a motivation would be self-centred rather than being self giving; a desire to love and serve Jesus.

Although many other religions have their hero figures, Christianity is unique in that its nature is one of a living, everlasting relationship with Jesus, the one who is both God and man. Whatever adherents to various religions may have in common in their systems of beliefs and moral codes, the one thing that inevitably must always differentiate them is the very nature of Christianity. Mere acknowledgement of Jesus as a great teacher, prophet and an exceptionally holy man is not the same thing as being bound to him in a mutual relationship of love.

It is absolutely clear as to what Christianity actually is. What remains is to understand what is the basis of the faith that allows that relationship to exist. It all rests on the conviction gained from experience that Jesus is as much alive and involved in life everywhere in the 21st century as he was in Palestine, two millennia ago. Friendship with him today differs from the friendship enjoyed by his contemporaries only is so far as he is not physically present with us now. But, to me, because through years of experience I have come gradually to know him better, his friendship is as real to me as the

16

friendship that I have had with people in different countries, some of whom I did not meet until many years after first getting to know them. Physical absence is no barrier to friendship and there is something in the saying that absence can make the heart grow fonder.

When we sing, 'What a friend we have in Jesus' we mean exactly that. He is not a hero whom we admire or worship; nor is he simply the ideal person whom we should like to be. Like any other friend, we interact, we listen, we speak; he listens and he acts. Pure friendship is most satisfying when we share sorrows or triumphs. As most Christians will witness, our friendship is most fruitful when we receive from him help and guidance to do things that we believe would be impossible if we were on our own.

That guidance and that help is what I understand is meant when we talk about the Grace of Our Lord Jesus Christ. That is why we conclude our prayers by saying, 'The Grace of Our Lord Jesus Christ, the love of God and the fellowship of the Holy Spirit be with us all evermore.' Grace is the quality of our relationship with Jesus. It is the greatest gift that any person can receive. Friendship with Jesus is priceless.

Chapter Three

The Historic Jesus

It is not the intention of this chapter to give a potted biography of Jesus of Nazareth. There are some good books which do that and help with an understanding of the Gospel stories that are our main sources of information on this extraordinary man. However, sometimes they can be more of a hindrance than a help if they have been written by someone who is keen to recruit Jesus in support of some cause. In recent years, he has even been portrayed as a patron saint of violent freedom fighters.

A book that I have found most useful is not a conventional biography, although in its last three chapters it tells us the essentials of the story with a clarity that would be difficult to surpass. It is by C H Dodd, who was Director of The New English Bible, and it is called *The Founder of Christianity* (Collins). Although it is written by a great scholar, it is a work of beautiful simplicity. It introduces the reader to the strange and distant world of life in Palestine two thousand years ago and deals with the outlook of the oppressed people of Israel and how they related to the Greek and Roman world. In the middle of the book, there are two illuminating chapters which deal with the personal traits of Jesus and with Jesus the teacher. They provide a dimension that is not always clear in a straight biography on Jesus.

When I meet someone that I want to get to know well, I particularly wish to find out what we may have in common. On the whole, it is easier if the person does not have a family background too dissimilar to my own. It also helps if they have similar occupations and interests. I am looking for someone that I can look upon as a companion rather than as a hero. For friendship and fellowship I must be confident about what it is that makes a person tick; what are dominant principles and motives. There are other qualities that I would expect most other people to share with me. If the friendship is to be real there must be mutual confidence and openness. This depends on honesty and truthfulness with one another. It often requires courage to tell the truth to a friend, and when the truth hurts there is always a need for sensitivity and sympathy. Often, a sharing of the hurt – compassion – is needed. It is often said that for a relationship to be fruitful, there must be give and take. Each has something to give to the other on a basis of mutuality. Such an exchange can be difficult if one partner is exceptional and the other is rather ordinary.

Our first meeting with Jesus as a friend is somewhat like getting acquainted with a pen friend. We depend upon the written word and initial impressions are very hazy. Although they improve, we often find that there have been misconceptions on the way and when we at last come face to face with our friend we are no longer entirely dependent on the written word. Of course, it can help if we have words not only directly from our friend, but we also learn from other people that have personal knowledge of him or her. The common experience of millions of people throughout the ages that Jesus is alive today helps reinforce one's own personal experience that grows with the passing of the years as we get to know him better. The written words are still important, but their meaning is clarified, interpreted and enriched.

After many years of friendship with Jesus I can see how the

Gospel stories reveal a surprising amount, not only about the teaching, but also the character and the personality of the man that corresponds with the experience derived from personal relationship.

The Man

As a child, Jesus was presented to me as an heroic person, with emphasis on the wonders that he performed. Whilst it is true that he possessed remarkable healing talents and a penetrating and perceptive insight, it is his normality rather than his egregiousness that now impresses me most. His family background was quite ordinary – the son of a carpenter. As an engineer myself I can feel a natural affinity with him on that level. I believe we pay far too little attention to the fact that he spent about seven times as long working at the bench as he did in his concluding public ministry. His experience no doubt contributed greatly to the concrete, earthy imagery in the pictures and stories that he used when speaking to the people. He never used the abstractions that are so much the stock in trade of academic theologians. As a busy tradesman, he would have had no time to waste in lengthy, complicated arguments.

This may to some extent explain how it was that his utterances were so direct, pithy, short and sometimes cryptic. Anyone who has worked for years at a bench knows that there is plenty of time for reflection, particularly if you feel an affinity with the materials you are using and the changes that take place as the object of your work takes shape. In so many of the illustrations that Jesus used, you can see

21

evidence of that kind of reflection. He saw ordinary, commonplace, trivial things and actions as sources of profound meaning and truth. To him, the whole world of things; plants, animals and people, was a school of lessons about meaning and God's purposes. In spite of his profound wisdom there is something delightfully unsophisticated about him that is very attractive. He displayed a simple sense of awe and wonder at the beauty and mystery of nature under the loving care of his Heavenly Father, The Creator and Sustainer of all things.

But how did he – how does he – relate to people? He obviously treated everyone with equal consideration and respect. In his story about the dishonest servant, he evidently considered that we can even learn something from the way scoundrels behave. Indeed, he was often criticised by those people that are more selective in those with whom they associate, for his practice of consorting with 'publicans and sinners' – even the despised tax collectors, the lackeys of the occupying power.

But there was nothing of the 'gentle Jesus, meek and mild' about him. He was a model of humility, but he made it clear that he had no time for shallow piety, or for smug self righteousness, as witness the attitude of the superior elder brother in the parable of the Prodigal Son and the story of the lawyers and the adulteress. It was always the sin, rather than the sinner, the hypocrisy, rather than the hypocrite, that aroused his anger.

However, he could be forthright in his judgements and sometimes even harsh, particularly when he was pitting his judgement against the authorities. Although it was a very dangerous thing to do, he showed great moral courage on such occasions. The fact that he was so cool and polite probably only heightened the impact on those he was criticising.

Although his knowledge, understanding and insight mark Jesus out as a clever person, he never flaunted his cleverness. In responding to enquirers he displayed gentle wisdom instead of cleverness. He encouraged and helped people to answer their own questions, often posing fictitious equivalent problems that depersonalised the real problem. The question, 'What must I do to inherit eternal life?' that was put to him on one occasion, was just such a question. Jesus replies, 'What is your reading of the law?' The reply is, 'Love God and your neighbour.' Jesus answers with the story of the Good Samaritan, ending with another question, 'Which of the three was neighbour to the injured man?' 'The one that showed him kindness,' replied the lawyer. 'Go and do as he did,' replied Jesus.

By helping people to discover the truth for themselves Jesus enhances their integrity and self respect. He never patronised, but helped people to take responsibility instead of becoming dependent. When they showed that they were unable to make a hard decision – as when he told the rich man to, 'Sell everything and give to the poor, then come and follow me.' – he did not chide, but showed sympathy; 'How hard it is to enter the Kingdom of God.'

In his other dealings with people, when he was responding to some need, although he was sensitive and compassionate, he was also unsentimental. As far as possible, he preferred to do things with people, calling on their trust, cooperation and involvement, rather than merely doing things for them. He was not a do-gooder. He wanted to produce courage and strength in people at the same time as inspiring confidence and trust in God rather than in himself. At times, if someone that was seeking his help did not respond sufficiently, but appeared to be too

23

dependent, Jesus could be quite brusque. Remember how he said to the bed-ridden man, 'Do you want to recover? If so, pick up your bed and walk.'

Of course, there was a note of authority in such a remark. Despite the fact that he was a very ordinary carpenter of Nazareth with no position or office to rely upon, there is no doubt that his authority was there for all to see. It was moral authority that he possessed. People believed him when he said, 'Your sins are forgiven you.' That was not merely a word of comfort, it was a challenge to go and do good – and they went. For one who was possessed of such moral authority, he was very sparing and humble in its application. Although he would say at times to some of his friends, 'I say unto you,' which, in modern parlance is something like, 'You can take it from me,' he was careful to disclaim any personal authority with sayings like, 'I do nothing on my own authority; all that I say I have been taught by my father.' But that disclaimer only added to the weight of what he was saying or doing.

Such strength of moral authority, linked with his fearless courage and honesty, inevitably put mortal fear into the establishment, so much so that it was inevitable that he would be killed so long as he did not betray his principles and his mission. He was obviously totally dedicated to his task and his humanity shows when, in sheer frustration, he exclaims, 'What an unbelieving and perverse generation! How long must I endure you.' It is clear from some of the comments made to him by even his closest friends that they had very little understanding of what he was doing or saying. He must have felt intensely lonely, perhaps most of all when surrounded by the crowds that came to see, hear and touch him. It must have been that sense of loneliness that made him seek periods of retreat and refreshment to be in intimate contact with God his Father, who alone knew and fully understood.

Simple, modest and unsophisticated as he was, here was someone without power or wealth or position who had a magnetic personality. In the words of C H Dodd, 'In the presence of Jesus, the dark forces which ravage the souls and bodies of men, were overcome and their victims made new.' Yet his essential message was so demanding of people – to give up entirely all their self-centredness – and so revolutionary that he suffered the fate of all extremists. Many heard the call but few responded to it; especially when he did not turn out to be the great national leader that they yearned for to free them from the Roman yoke. Before we can be sure that we want to grasp the hand of his friendship, we must try to understand what is the essence of his revolutionary message, so that we can know what the effect of such a friendship is likely to be. Friendship with revolutionaries can be very costly and dangerous.

The Teacher

I have said that the picture of Jesus I had as a child was very different than the one I now have as a result of three things – reading and re-reading the Gospel stories for myself, reading and hearing the description given by other people of their own experiences, and, lastly, my own personal experience of a long and enriching relationship with him in prayer and thought and action. There is just a big gulf between what came to me as a young person of the teaching of Jesus and what I now perceive to be the essence of his teaching ministry. What I find very puzzling indeed is how seldom one does hear the central message that Jesus proclaimed mentioned by the Church today – the coming of God's kingdom into the world. God's intervention into history was for the purposes of introducing an entirely new spiritual order into the material world and in which a new intimate relationship between the creator and his creation was formed though a rebirth of Spirit. Because we have not grasped that truth, we continue to think and perceive things in secular terms instead of through the eye of the Spirit.

If you went into the centre of any town or village in Britain today and said the words that Jesus said over and over again – 'The time has come; the Kingdom of God is upon you.' People would probably nod their heads and look sorry for you. To the people of Galilee or Jerusalem two thousand years ago, it obviously had a big impact because they said to one another, 'He is a prophet, like one of the old prophets.' They must have had a fairly clear idea of what he meant.

Put into our own language and contemporary setting, it seems to have meant something like, 'We have been living through a long period during which the whole of our lives have been governed by rules and regulations given by God through Moses and the prophets. Now the point has been reached when God is giving the whole of his creation a new start. This age is to be one on which God's own spirit is coming to help us escape from out inbuilt self-centredness, so that we can live gloriously as free men and women, free communities and nations. We are no longer to be left like helpless children living confined lives according to the do's and don'ts of the Law. There is no suggestion that the laws don't matter. We shall be wise to remember the help that they have been in living decently and responsibly. The difference is that we shall be guided by the Spirit of God to live life abundantly by caring for one another and making good judgements, rather than in the strait jacket of the Law.'

The particular laws at the time of Jesus were very different from the laws under which we live. Today we are governed more by the laws of mammon than by the laws of Moses and the prophets. But that does not in any way invalidate the central message of Jesus. Like all people throughout history, we have our lives shaped by rules and regulations. Our situation is worse than that of the Israelites because we are governed by systems that are manmade. All the pressures are for keeping to the letter of those laws. It is the letter that is so deadening. If only we could be free to act responsibly and kindly to one another.

When Paul was writing to the Christians in Corinth (2 Corinthians, chapter 3) he was addressing people whose lives were shaped by a different set of laws to those of the Jews. Nevertheless, he saw no problem in proclaiming the same message that Jesus delivered to the people of Palestine, because the Law of Love is universal and knows no boundaries. He drives home the point by saying that 'the written law brings death (because by it we are all condemned) but the Spirit gives life.' He then goes on to say that it is only when a person has surrendered his or her life to Christ, allowing the spirit to cooperate in and through that person, that freedom is gained. 'The capacity that we have (to live as free men and women) comes from God; it is he who made us capable of living in the new order of things, which consists not of a written law but of the Spirit.' It is that knowledge that gives assurance and makes Christians bold.

This message that Jesus brought to his contemporaries is one to all peoples at all times. In every generation everywhere we need to be set free to become what we are meant to be – fully adult responsible human beings in a living relationship with God. This new order of the Spirit is a marvellous challenge to us individually and corporately to live in harmony with one another with the help and inspiration of The Holy Spirit. The proclamation of a new created order was not something that could be left even to a prophet as great as Moses. It was not a new set of rules to be carved in stone or put on a computer, it was a living message that had to be demonstrated as well as being described in words and pictures. It was a message which only God himself could deliver by entering into the human situation in the person of Jesus of Nazareth. It was through his life, death and resurrection that the new order was begun, demonstrated and made effective for all. Jesus once said, 'If by the finger of God I drive out devils, then be sure that the Kingdom of God has come upon you.'

In a sense, it was the Incarnation that produced the crisis that is a continuing turning point in every age. Inevitably, it introduced a decision and a judgement from which there is no escape. There is no compulsion to abandon the childish living of life by the Law. The history of the last two thousand years suggests that, despite the influence of the Church, the challenge to live by the Spirit has been exceptional rather than general. We continue to put our faith in ourselves and our ability to shape our own destiny, rather than recognising that we can only be capable of living well by surrendering control to the Spirit of God and depending upon him alone.

Happily, there are innumerable examples of individual lives that confirm the truth of the reality of the new covenant between God and man. God does keep his promises. Nobody can say that it was a marvellous idea, but unfortunately it was impractical. What is clear is that the new life that reflects the quality of the life of Jesus is lived by people who have made a total surrender and commitment to Him. This does not imply that the only good lives are those that are lived by Christian saints. There are many examples of good lives that are lived by people who are not Christians, but only total surrender to the Spirit of God can transform the most unpromising life and turn it into a faithful representation of the life of Jesus. The great paradox is that we gain freedom by surrendering self-will and, in doing so, we take responsibility for ourselves and for our neighbours and for the environment. The life and the sayings of Jesus are the supreme example of a God-centred, Spirit-filled existence that knows no bounds of time and place, and is not even confined to this life on earth.

It has to be said that the coming of the Kingdom – the new order – inevitably creates a judgement for every person that is faced with the Incarnation, Crucifixion and Resurrection. There could be no greater demonstration of God's love for his creation. None can escape the need to respond in thankfulness and love when they hear the words of Jesus, 'It is not the will of your Father that one of these little ones should be lost.'

Through the unique historical event of 'God with us', mankind is brought face to face with the love of the creator of all things, who is supreme, good and almighty in power, yet gentle and tender in his goodness; forgiving and totally loving in his power towards every speck of his creation.

To someone who has lived at a time when the unity of all creation has gained a new meaning through the development of the science of ecology, the truth that Jesus revealed has a special impact and significance. It is the whole of creation, not only the human race, that is the object of God's love. 'God so loved the world...' If men and women are changed by submission to the inspiration of the Holy Spirit, the effects will be felt throughout all creation. The new creation of everything is a mystery that no doubt means much more than that, but it certainly does not mean any less.

Although the Incarnation once and for all demonstrated that in this world the material and the spiritual are inseparable, Jesus, through his teaching, his life, death and resurrection, leaves us in no doubt that the new creation is not confined to life on earth. It begins here, in the here and now, but progresses into a new phase beyond the grave. Because of the glorious resurrection of Jesus, it is more than a mere hope; it is a certainty. It is the source of meaning and purpose in life. Without the Resurrection, we are without hope, as Paul reminded the Christians at Corinth. With it, we can make sense of life and death. Thus the proclamation and the presence of the Kingdom through Jesus not only introduces a new way of living here on earth, it also contains the certain promise of a life of ongoing fellowship with him in the presence of the loving Father of creation.

Because of this marvellous revelation, the Orthodox Christian greeting 'Christ is risen' and the response, 'He is risen indeed' are charged with the most profound meaning and significance. I wonder that it is not the universal Christian greeting. Likewise, the phrase, 'May the body and blood of Christ keep you in life eternal' assures us that we are in fellowship with Christ partaking mysteriously of spiritual refreshment through the inspiration of the Holy Spirit of God.

A fundamental part of the teaching of Jesus concerning the Kingdom is that new life is dependent on unconditional forgiveness of all who have harmed us. This is evident in many parts of the Gospel story. The parable of the unmerciful servant (Matthew, chapter 18, verse 23) points out that forgiveness is a two - way thing; it has to be given before it can be received. Neither the forgiving nor the receiving of forgiveness are necessarily easy and in some instances they can be almost impossible. Reconciliation requires a genuine change of heart and attitude on the part of the one needing forgiveness and generosity on the part of the giver. There is no way that forgiveness can be earned. God's forgiveness is unlimited but it is qualified by the need for a genuine change of heart.

The impossibility of earning forgiveness is one of the revolutionary features of the Kingdom of God. Another such feature relates to justice in the kingdom, in contrast with our ideas of human justice. The parable of the workers in the vineyard gives an example of what appears to be manifest injustice. It drives home the point that, under the sovereignty of God, his sovereign generosity cannot be circumscribed by any set of rules, even the laws of natural justice. It is unlimited.

Paradoxically, Jesus, the Incarnate Son of God, is undeniably the Servant King who washes the feet of his most lowly subjects. God is a God of unlimited power and authority, but also a God of infinite love, generosity and forgiveness.

Before going further, we must first examine some of the central claims that Jesus made about himself, his nature, his mission and his relationship with God. It is only in the light of such an examination that conclusions can be drawn which will reveal to us the significance that we must attach to his reported sayings. But before coming to his claims, there is just one more thing to be said about Jesus.

Those friends who were closest to him were Jewish monotheists, schooled in the belief of only one true God. The idea of worshipping a human being was totally abhorrent to them. Nevertheless, so transparent was the divinity of Jesus – goodness personified, with powers such as no man had either before or since – that they pray to him as a God, not as their hero leader. He alone is worthy of worship because he is God with us.

His Claims

Most religious teachers have been very modest, self-effacing individuals. Perhaps the most extraordinary thing about Jesus, even to the extent of being shocking, was that he talked about himself and made many extraordinary claims. As William Temple put it, 'The one Christ for whom there is any evidence is a miraculous figure making stupendous claims.' A puzzling aspect of the claims is the contrast with the emphasis that he put into his teaching on the virtue of humility. In a way, that paradox is one of the things that tends to substantiate his claims, for had they not convinced his friends of their truth, they surely would have wanted nothing to do with someone who, on the one hand, preached humility, yet on the other, made stupendous claims to have a unique relationship with God. It was not surprising that the religious establishment considered him to be guilty of blasphemy. Had his repeated assertion not been self-evidently feasible to those with whom he was most intimate, could he have possibly survived so long the anger that such utterances would inevitably produce?

Here are some such claims:

'I am the way, the truth and the life; no-one comes to the Father but by me.'

'I am the light of the world; he who follows me will not walk in darkness but have the light of life.'

'I am the bread of life; he who comes to me shall not hunger and he who believes in me shall never thirst.'

'I am the resurrection and the life; he who believes in me though he were yet dead shall he live and whoever lives and believes in me shall never die.'

Just as shocking were the direct references to his unique relationship with God, the Creator and Sustainer of all things;

'I and the Father are one. I am in the Father and the Father is in me.'

He assumed the Messianic title, 'Son of Man' and, when challenged by the High Priest, he accepted the title 'Son of God'. Perhaps the most momentous remarks are those recorded by Matthew in verse 27 of chapter 11;

'All things have been delivered to me by my Father, and no-one knows the Son except the Father and no-one knows the Father except the Son and anyone to whom the Son chooses to reveal him.'

Could any claim be more exclusive, or more blasphemous, if it was not true?

There were more claims, all of which reinforced his main claim to be 'God made man'. He did not say, as did the prophets of, 'Thus saith the Lord.' Jesus said, 'Truly, truly I (repeat, I) say to you.' What he said was so different and so authoritative that, 'the crowds were astonished at his teaching, for he taught them as one who has authority.' His claim to forgive sin shocked religious leaders but the subjects of his forgiveness jumped for joy at the liberation that his forgiveness gave them.

But his claims were not only assertions. He demonstrated their truth by innumerable acts of healing and love, all of which were charged with spiritual significance. Words and deeds together cannot easily be denied.

However, had it not been for his final act of resurrection he might still have gone down in history as most extraordinary, but possibly a demented genius, despite the coincidence of his words and deeds. It would seem that even though Peter and some of his other close friends believed him to be the Son of God, his death by crucifixion undermined that conviction. It was the Resurrection that restored their faith and set them up to continue his work.

The Resurrection, which Jesus has announced to his disciples in advance, sets the seal on all the extraordinary claims that Jesus made for himself and his relationship with God the Father. It is the truth of these claims that Jesus made for himself and for his relationship with God the Father. It is the truth of these claims that gives the answer to the question that must be asked of any great body of teaching; 'Is there anything special about this teacher that makes his teaching superior to all others?' Although he was a mere carpenter of Nazareth, who did not produce anything comparable with the learned works of classical philosophers and religious writers, his teaching stands alone because, as he himself said, 'I am the way, the truth and the life; no-one comes to the Father but by me.'

His claims about himself, particularly concerning his relationship with God, cannot be separated from his teaching,. They are together God's revelation to mankind through the Incarnation and Resurrection. I find the idea that he was only one of the greatest moral teachers of all time quite ridiculous. How could such a megalomaniac be such a great teacher if there were no truth in his claims?

As Sir Stafford Cripps once said in a broadcast, 'Jesus was either bad or mad or who he said he was.' We only have two choices about Jesus of Nazareth; either we totally reject him as a demented charlatan and impostor, or we totally accept him for what he claimed himself to be, with all that this implies. I can see no contradiction in his character, his teaching or his claims and actions that leave me in any doubt.

His Promises Bequests and Legacy

In Chapters 13 to 17 of John's gospel we can read his account of the final conversation Jesus had with his disciples at the last supper before he surrendered himself to the authorities. Jesus tells them what is going to happen. Because it will be very distressing for them, he reassures them that he will return to them for a time, so that their shattered faith can be restored and they can see that death has been conquered. Then, when he finally returns to his father God, he will prepare for them to join him forever when they die.

During his talk, he gives them a new commandment to love one another as he has loved them. Jesus is calling for something much more difficult than the old commandment to love your neighbour as yourself, It is to treat each other selflessly, sacrificially, compassionately and forgiving everything. He knows this is humanly impossible. Nevertheless, he expects it of them, because he promises them that God will send his Spirit to guide, help and empower them whenever they ask, so what seems impossible becomes possible and gradually their lives will be transformed, becoming like his.

But this is not the only amazing gift that he promises if they ask God. He says he will not be asking God on their behalf, but promises that, because of their love for him, they can make their requests to God direct and not through any intermediary.

There surely could be no greater gifts than the promise of a Helper to enable anyone who asks to overcome their human defects and limitations and also, amazingly, to be able to talk to God and directly ask for help.

To know God is to know what God is like and to have a living relationship with Him. Through Jesus, we know what God is like, and because of Jesus and his loving self sacrifice, we receive the greatest honour of living with God in our daily lives. Consequently, we are able to experience the truth of the promises which Jesus made, like millions of others over two thousand years. But in addition to these personal bequests, there is another legacy which is given. When members of communities put their faith into practice, the environment in which they live is transformed as 'the law of love' becomes embedded. By this means, over the centuries, the world has been given an immense inheritance. Hospitals, universities and schools have all been inspired and born where Christianity has taken root. The English language, which in many ways is becoming worldwide in terms of usage, has been greatly enriched by Christian literature. Similarly, most of the greatest works of art and architecture and music from the western world have been inspired by Christianity and much of modern science, engineering and technology has been developed within countries where Christianity flourished.

All this, and more, is evidence that, 'God so loved the world.'

Chapter Four

The Contemporary Jesus

Because all that we can learn about the 'historic' Jesus is so fundamentally important, there is a danger that we pay insufficient attention to the Jesus who is still active in the world, even though he is not present in the flesh. The story of his life in Palestine runs, for, at most, three years. The story of the resurrected Jesus whose Spirit continues to live in all who have invited him into their lives has lasted for two thousand years. It is a story that embodies the truth of his prophetic assertion that those who followed after him would perform even greater deeds than he had done himself.

When I was a young Christian, I was eager to read about the wonders that the Spirit had worked over the centuries following the extraordinary happenings of the first Pentecost. I expected to find them in Church histories, but was very disappointed. However, when I turned to biographies of great historic Christian figures, I found what I was looking for. These were lives – sometimes very unpromising lives to begin with – totally transformed after they were unreservedly committed to God's will and selfish ambition was abandoned. Some of the ones that impressed me most were little known, ordinary people who, with little or no support, ventured alone to take the Good News to distant corners of the earth, whose faith and trust was rewarded in what can only be described as miraculous ways.

Most people have some idea of what constitutes a miracle. Possibly these days the commonest idea is that a miracle is something very unusual that has no rational explanation and which seems not to fit in with conventional scientific wisdom. For some strange reason, people do not generally consider the creation of life in the Universe to be particularly miraculous, despite the fact that there is an extraordinary combination of coincidence, without which life could not possibly have come into existence. For example, gravitational force is one of several key forces that are basic and universal in their action. If the strength of the gravitational force was only slightly more or less, by a minute amount, than it is, then life could not exist.

The same thing applies to the fundamental forces of nature – such as nuclear and electromagnetic . For life to exist, each one needs to be precisely what it is. The likelihood that these coincidences could have happened by chance seems to be to be very slight indeed. The improbability must, at least, prompt the question, 'is there not some deliberate design intention that accounts for this extraordinary coincidence?'

Before scientists revealed these facts and their implications for the existence of life on earth, it seems to me and to many other people that the processes of nature are so subtle and complex that it is more difficult to imagine that they exist by chance rather than being a product of intelligent design, far greater than any of human origin. The difficulties that human beings experience in trying to unravel the workings of nature is a witness to that. For me, the whole creative evolutionary process is by far the biggest miracle of all. Every other inexplicable, unnatural event, no matter how extraordinary it may seem, pales into insignificance by comparison. They can only be described as minor miracles against the major miracle of creation.

Because we believe that science has provided a fairly reliable understanding of the regular laws of nature and what fits or does not fit into that framework, there is inevitably a tendency to dismiss events that do not appear to fit, rather than admit that they are mysterious. Life seems simpler if mystery is outlawed. Professor Ray Peacock, a prominent physical scientist and aeronautical engineer, has been forced to conclude that the physical results of faith-healing that he has observed are inexplicable other than as a consequence of the influence of Christian prayer. His acceptance followed an intellectual struggle that forced him to recognise that, whereas in scientific investigation, trust is only possible when no observations are inconsistent with accepted theoretical understanding, in the operation of the spiritual realm an event occurs only as a consequence of conviction and total trust that it can occur mysteriously and contrary to normal expectation. In a world that is uncomfortable with mystery, it is very difficult for many people to comprehend the workings of the spiritual realm.

Faith-healing by no means always produces the results that are prayed for; nevertheless, there are innumerable instances where the consequences are totally unexpected and contrary to normal expectations according to conventional scientific understanding. But physical miracles, although great in number as a result of Christian prayer, are few compared with other kinds of non-physical happenings which can only be understood in terms of activity of the Spirit in God in human affairs. In a world of hundreds of millions of praying Christians there must be millions of such miraculous divine interventions that influence behaviour which are happening every day.

Each individual Christian, if they examine the consequences of

41

their own personal prayer life very carefully, will be able to recall many instances of significant divine intervention that have guided their actions.

But God's Holy Spirit is not limited to activity in and through the lives of Christians. He is comprehensively the source of all goodness. But it is through the followers of Jesus that we can claim that it is the Holy Spirit that Jesus promised to give us that is at work.

Jesus – the contemporary Jesus – not only lives, he is active all the time – past, present and future – everywhere. I know this to be true because I have experienced his influence over fifty years, in innumerable small ways and in a few major turning points in my life. Some of the most significant interventions are described below. The thing that makes me most certain that they are the result of divine intervention is that, in each case, I found myself moving in directions that were contrary to my personal wishes or inclinations.

I was just thirty years old, having a most enjoyable time doing exactly the things that I liked doing most as an Associate Director in Shell's laboratories in Cheshire. Then the call came to move to Head Office to help form a new product development department. I resisted for a while, then I gave way when I was given an assurance that I could return to the laboratory after eighteen months. At the end of that time, although I really wanted to go back, I knew in my heart that it was right that I should remain in London. That was a major turning point in my life that turned out to be a great blessing.

Nearly thirty years later I was approaching retirement, with exciting plans to do some research on the way that plants produce vegetable oils when I noticed an advertisement in my daily paper for a

Director of the Industrial Christian Fellowship. Something seemed to say to me, 'You ought to apply for that.' I quickly put the idea out of my mind. Several weeks later, it happened once again as I turned the pages of the paper when the job was readvertised. This time I was caught. I tried to argue my way out of it, partly because I felt ill equipped to do the job, but to no avail. I was appointed and my retirement plans had to be abandoned. But what a blessing that was. In previous jobs I had training and experience on which I could rely. This time, I was forced to rely entirely on God's guidance. 'How blessed are those who know their need of God.'

These are just two examples of divine intervention, in answer to prayer, that have happened over the years. There have been more; before and after I was thirty, and since I finally retired, after five years with the Industrial Christian Fellowship. Thank God that on each occasion the Holy Spirit prompted me to go against my personal inclinations. There were other occasions when I went my own way. The loss has been mine; such is the price of disobedience.

But there is more to the influence of the contemporary Jesus than changed individual lives. His influence can be seen in all forms of corporate life and in world development over the past two thousand years. When Christianity came to pagan Britain it gradually permeated all aspects of life on these islands and became the dominant influence for change in the social, intellectual and political spheres. Within the last few hundred years the same change processes have occurred in many new parts of the world to which the Gospel has been taken. Of course, this is not to say that wherever the influence of Christianity has gone, all that was bad has been replaced by things that conform to the

Christian ideal. That has not happened any more than it happens in the lives of individuals who embrace the Christian faith, But over time traditional ways of life are transformed.

As an engineer, I am impressed by the history of science and technology and, in particular, how developments in Christian countries have moved far ahead of all other parts of the world, until now their influence is worldwide, even in countries that are anti-Christian. There is a tendency to think that this had its origins in science in the seventeenth century, and in technology with the beginning of the Industrial Revolution in the eighteenth century. But Professor Lynn White Jnr. of the University of California has traced the origins of advance in Christian countries to very much earlier dates. It was in technological developments that advances of major significance were made. Until the seventeenth century, heavy soils could not be ploughed by 'scratch ploughs'. It was the introduction of a new kind of plough in Christian Europe, with its vertical knife to cut under the sod, and a mouldboard to turn it over, that revolutionised agriculture. About the same time water power, which hitherto had been used only to mill grain, began to be used for industrial purposes such as sawing timber and pumping furnace bellows in Christian Europe.

A distinctive Christian tradition of science did not appear until about the fourteenth century, after which it achieved world leadership when, as a branch of natural theology, it ceased to concern itself with interpreting nature as symbols of God's communication with mankind, and became an effort to understand the mind of God by discovering how his creation operates. For centuries, until comparatively recently, science was motivated by this religious quest. Even Isaac Newton considered himself as essentially a theologian and it was the dynamic of religious devotion that provided him with much of his impetus.

Perhaps it is significant that it is only since science and technology have been separated from this divine motivation, to become servants of mammon, that concerns have arisen about the damage being done to mankind and nature. Because of those concerns, there is a growing insistence that ethical considerations must be applied to all new developments. After 150 years of exclusion of the Christian Church from new scientific and technological debate, there is a new search for ethical wisdom in which Churches are being called upon to play a part. Like the Israelites during the Exodus, we have been wandering in the desert, refusing to submit to the demands of God, to acknowledge his sovereignty and to follow his directions. In the words of Psalm 95, we 'are a people that do err in their hearts because they have not known my ways.'

Not only is it the scientific quest in the Christian world to understand the mind of God by discovering how his creation works that is evidence of the activity of the Holy Spirit in the followers of Jesus. There are other unique expressions of the enlightening love of Jesus across a wide range of social and political changes. Perhaps, in the political sphere, the influence of great Christians like William Wilberforce in bringing about the abolition of slavery is the most dramatic.

Less spectacular, but of great importance, has been the development of movements for freedom and human rights. A reading of the UN Charter and the declaration of Human Rights is a singular expression of the commandment to, 'love one another' unconditionally.

45

But long before the signing of the UN Charter there have been many non-political expressions of the same caring for one another in Christian countries, with such organisation as the Christian Red Cross, the Salvation Army, a multiplicity of health, educational and social support organisations such as the Girls' Friendly Society, Scouts and Guides, the Trades Unions and Church-based bodies like Toc H, the YMCA, YWCA and the Boys' and Girls' Brigades. Although many have now spread to many parts of the world, including some non Christian countries, they all had their origins in Christian Europe, drawing their inspiration and strength from the power of the Holy Spirit of God in action with us and in us. There have been other great individuals who have had a profound influence on sections of mankind, but none can compare with Jesus whose activity throughout the ages is a consistent expression of the universal and unconditional love of God for all his creation. It is from God that all good things come.

For some people the immensely important evidences of the continuing activity in the world of the contemporary Jesus at work through the agency of his followers seems not to have the same impact as the comparatively rare instances of physical instances that defy scientific explanation and sometimes seem to contradict normality. Like many of the healing miracles that Jesus performed during his earthly ministry, most present day incidents concern faith-healing, when medical opinion is that there is no possible cure. Always the common factors are faith and fervent prayer.

One fairly recent example in Dorset involved a thirty five year old family man. He ran a driving school until a back problem put him in a wheelchair, when he was told he would never walk again. As a member of his Church congregation, he attended a summer camp at Post Green. He was on the stage in a group leading worship when one of the group began to speak in tongues. He says, 'I could not understand him, but I suddenly felt good. I still could not move my legs but all the pain had gone.' The completion occurred one morning later and he is now able to live an active physical life. 'Great,' says his son, 'Now we can play football together.'

This is only one instance among many. All have the same conviction that their new-found health is a gracious gift from God in answer to prayer. People who say that the recorded miracles of Jesus are fairy tales simply do not face the facts that they are still being performed by the contemporary Jesus.

From our 21st century perspective, the amazing healing that takes place every day through the application of medicine and surgery, to millions of people, does not appear to be miraculous, presumably because we think that we can understand how it has happened. Why should understanding make it any less miraculous? No doubt, it would have seemed miraculous at the time of Jesus – or even two hundred years ago. I wonder whether there is any real difference between healing by doctors, nurses and surgeons and what is described as faith-healing. In both cases, it is God's gracious gift, for which we give thanks, because in both cases healing cannot be guaranteed in advance. In every case of healing there has to be faith in the patient that healing is possible; and in many cases healing cannot be guaranteed in advance. In every case of healing there has to be faith in the patient that healing is possible and in many cases prayers are involved, and are not the skills and loving care in the practice of modern medicine themselves precious gifts from God?

When a specialist says, 'There is nothing more that I can do to cure you.' is he not simply saying that the limits of present day God given knowledge and skills has been reached, and only God, in his infinite knowledge and wisdom can help you if you put your faith in him? It is possible when Jesus said to the disciples, 'You will perform even greater miracles than I have done' he was prophesying that God would, in due course, give new knowledge and skills that would enable future generations to do things that were unimaginable to them?

Although we have these many evidences of Jesus alive today, and very active in the world working through the agency of his devoted followers, it is not through these things alone that we come to know and understand the Lord of all life. Two millennia of experience simply confirms that the work begun by Jesus in Palestine continues to be done all over the world in the way that he promised. But the witness consensus is, as it has always been, that it is through a prayerful, reflective reading of the Scriptures and a commitment to follow him that his followers get to know him and to understand what are his unchanging purposes. We are only able to understand the contemporary Jesus if we get to know, through the record of his life on earth, the historic Jesus. They are one. It is not enough to know about Jesus from Scripture and from his present activity. You only know Jesus when you experience his activity within your own life.

The contemporary Jesus may be ignored for a while, but ultimately, his will must prevail in all spheres of life because in the final analysis only love can prevail. Although in our arrogance and ignorance, 'we have erred and strayed from God's ways like lost sheep', a Christian believes that it is possible for mankind to 'modify his instruments to the pattern of his reverence'. But for the accomplishment of this transforming task, we must recover a true reverence, be unconditionally committed to seek his will and do it at all costs in fellowship with him. It is a task to discover God through a right relationship with each other and through our right use of God's gifts. We cannot achieve one without the other; and both, if they are to be successful, require obedience to God and his purposes. It is a modern illusion that a good society and a thriving economy can be based merely on a human centred, money driven, worldly purpose. 'Seek first the Kingdom of God and his righteousness and all these things shall be added unto you.'

We stand in a mess at the dawn of a new era and our question is, 'What are we to do to make the world decently habitable for all the billions of us?' When the disciples asked Jesus the same sort of question, 'What shall we do that we may work the works of God?' his reply was simply, 'This is the work of God, that you believe in him whom he has sent.' Only by trusting him and following his example and guidance can we be empowered to overcome our crippling self centredness that is the root cause of all our problems. We must live in him and he in us.

'By their fruits shall ye know them.' Those who put their trust in God can produce the good that corresponds to God's will and intention for his creation. Only by following Jesus, inspired and empowered by the Holy Spirit, can the world become decently habitable for all of us. Hans Kung describes a Christian person or community as, 'one for whom Jesus Christ is ultimately decisive ... Christianity only exists where the memory of Jesus is activated in theory and in practice.'

When all people and all communities have Jesus as the one who is, for them, ultimately decisive, and who activate his memory through practice can the mess that we are in be transformed into the world that is for the Glory of God and the fulfilment of His Kingdom.

Chapter Five

What is it that only Jesus can give us?

There is so much on offer in modern society, competing for our attention, that it is only natural that people should wonder whether there can be anything unique which only Jesus is able to provide that is of great importance.

Is it not odd that, after centuries in which God was seen as the key to life, in our generation God is largely ignored in old Christian countries? Perhaps one among many reasons is that there are so many false images of God imprinted on people's minds.

Some of these false images were implanted in early childhood and have never been erased. Our Father in Heaven seemed to be an invisible figure who constantly kept an eye on you, noting every slip, whose main purpose seemed to be to stop you from enjoying yourself. That fearful image of God was confused by another you were led to believe would do your bidding if you asked him in your prayers, but who never seemed to be listening when you did ask. Another early and potentially dangerous image was of an angry and powerful being whose approval you had to seek by strenuous efforts of doing good.

More confusions set in later at school and at church. Strange pictures of God in the Old Testament were of a powerful being who put curses on some people and made favourites of others; who demanded the practice of very peculiar rituals and unpleasant sacrifices. In contrast, in many of the Psalms and in other parts of the Bible, God is portrayed as entirely loving, just and trustworthy, deserving of reciprocal love and worship.

It is only when we are introduced to Jesus, who claims to be sent as a manifestation of God, that we can see a true but partial picture of what God is really like. In nobody else, and nowhere else, can we find such a true likeness of the One who is the Creator and Sustainer of all things and all life. This is the first supremely important thing that Jesus gives us.

The false image of a tyrannical God was alienating. It was impossible to respect, let alone love and worship such a God. Little wonder that the Israelites so frequently turned to worship other gods. The only possible corrective to such a grossly distorted picture was a living revelation in human form which, through character and action, could provide a partial but true glimpse of what God is really like. Jesus is uniquely that living revelation. It is only through him that we can see a divine nature which can attract us all to love God 'with all our hearts, with all our minds, with all our souls and with all our strength.'

So we can now see something of what God is like, and that is splendid. However, it still leaves God there and us here with all our innermost longings to be with him. No matter how well things are, it seems that nothing on earth can fully satisfy us. At times, we may be hardly aware of it when we are caught up in daily life. Then it does not bother us much. At other times it feels as though everything is futile and nothing really matters. Longing and emptiness rises and falls but it never completely disappears. We are left wondering what can be done at the root of our dissatisfaction and how we can be fulfilled.

Could it be that a sense of our personal limitations frustrates us and makes us feel inadequate? In my own case, I feel that my two most important, inbuilt limitations were low self-esteem and self-centredness. Completely to overcome both of these two handicaps would perhaps liberate me from my frustration. In my own experience I am convinced that it has been the influence of the Holy Spirit within me, which Jesus promised to send, that alone has helped me to break both of these limitations.

Low self-esteem and self-centredness affect all parts of life. The area in which it is easiest to describe my experience is my career. As a boy I longed to be an engineer. Such was my sense of inadequacy that I could not see myself becoming anything more than a draughtsman. My performance at school was so mediocre that I never dreamed of going to university, so I left school and became an apprentice. Whilst there, something unexpectedly prompted me to sit for University scholarship which, surprisingly, I won. I can only explain my action, which was quite contrary to my poor self-esteem, as evidence of the prompting of the Holy Spirit.

All through my career in industry, and after, I have found myself doing things far beyond my wildest expectations. As an engineer, I have received the highest award of my peers, as a fellow of the Royal Academy of Engineering. As a young man, I had no idea of ever becoming a businessman. Nevertheless, by the age of 45, I found myself as the Head of Marketing in one of the biggest companies in the world. Since I was 50, I have been involved successfully in a series of totally unexpected activities for which I was seriously ill prepared.

At every step along the way I have been carried progressively further and further beyond the boundaries that I earlier perceived to be my limits. Often, because I felt that I was being taken out of my depth,

I put up quite stiff resistance; despite that, I was taken forward into unknown territory. In retrospect, I am confident that it was the influence of the Holy Spirit that was liberating me from my low self-esteem, lack of confidence and self-centredness.

The reason why I include self-centredness is that, whereas at the beginning of my career my main motivation was self-satisfaction, as the years passed I found myself increasingly unconcerned about my personal interests and more and more outward looking. Extending the boundaries of my life was a change at a secular level brought about by the action of the Spirit of Jesus within me. But that same Spirit operates at another, deeper level – the spiritual inner core of my being – transforming my self-centredness into an outgoing, self-sacrificial caring kind of love. The material prizes that I received as my career progressed proved to be of surprisingly little consequence. When the time came to relinquish them, I discovered how little they meant to me. The greatest satisfaction I have comes from doing whatever it was that I felt I was being called to do, even when there was no material or other secular recognition.

Nevertheless, it would be false to say that no trace of self centeredness remains. It is a powerful force which makes its presence felt when I am not alert to the tempting influence of pride and greed. One occasion when I most strongly felt the tug of the self was the time when I believed that I should abandon my main career at 50, just as I was beginning to enjoy the fruits of all that had gone before. On every side I knew that friends and colleagues thought that I was barmy, whether or not they told me so. Until I had passed the point of no return, there were many thoughts like, 'Is it fair to my family?' that made me waver in my conviction. Such thoughts seem selfless enough, but I knew that there was in them more than an element of unwillingness on my part to give up all the enjoyable and satisfying things that I was about to leave for no reason other than a conviction that it was the right thing to do. It was not that I was attached to something that I expected would be more rewarding than what I was leaving. However, although my decision to abandon my main career has not provided the same kind of satisfactions that I previously enjoyed, their loss has been more than compensated by even greater satisfactions of a different kind. I have, in fact, enjoyed life more abundantly.

In retirement, as I begin to grow old and physical and mental signs of decay begin to set in, the strange and exciting transforming power of Jesus begins to operate at the same spiritual level but in a different way. Surprisingly ageing does not seem to matter. Instead, there is a joyful sense of liberation as physical things, which have placed so many demands on you, fade. There is no longer any need to plan and scheme. Life is altogether more carefree and can be lived with spontaneity. Frustration from personal limitations and self-centredness may have accounted, in part, for earlier unsatisfied longings, now, most of all, it is a desire for a loving relationship that is free from the limitations of all human relationships - even the best of them – that becomes the priority. We come closest to that perfection in the best of marriages; I know because I have been blessed in that way. I can now see the depth of meaning in the notion that the Church is the Bride of Christ.

The relationship with Jesus is even more perfect and more desirable, because it is not constrained by any human limitation. The greatest blessing of ageing is that there is a freedom to develop that relationship without distraction. It will reach perfection with physical death, when self-centredness is finally put to rest.

The supreme gift which Jesus alone gives us is an entry into such a completely satisfying and fulfilling relationship – a relationship that places no demands on us, that is ever present, unconditional, full of active goodwill and everlasting. Nothing on earth can provide such a blessing that cannot be broken by death. All earthly things are conditional, variable and temporary. The friendship of Jesus is unconditional, constant and permanent, beyond time and space, available to all; a priceless gift no matter how unworthy we may be to receive it.

What a friend we have in Jesus – who is alive and active – I in him and he in me.

What must we give back to God?

The unique things that Jesus offers to everyone are gifts from God, freely and lovingly given. They are priceless, and they automatically create a loving response in gratitude from people who recognise them for what they are and accept them. Everyone whose inner eye is opened to begin to know Jesus through experience testifies to a desire to do only those things that please God. The more they experience Jesus as a present and active force in their lives, the more does self-centredness give way to God-centredness. The thing that the modern disciple wants to do, above everything else, is to follow the Good Shepherd and become an active part of the Body of Christ, continuing the good work that Jesus started two thousand years ago.

In both word and action, Jesus made clear what that work is. He calls upon his followers to, above all, care for one another; to heal the sick, give hope to the poor, and relief to all who, in one way or another, are in need. The sight of the Love of God in action, as exemplified by Jesus, is what will attract men and women, boys and girls, to a life of faith and love and fulfilment. The mission of every friend of Jesus is to continue his work 'with all their heart, with their mind, with their soul and with all their strength'. This is true evangelism.

Knowing about Jesus is important, but, as is clear from history, it is not enough to make a real difference. Only direct personal experience of the Living Jesus can do that, and that experience comes to faithful, trusting followers who, with the inspiration and power of prayer, seek to do only those things which please God and which are the mission of Jesus.

In the first chapter, we saw that every society needs a social glue that binds everyone and everything together in order to give it stability and cohesion. For centuries, Christianity provided that glue in Britain; not as a body of dogma or ideology, but as a devotion to the person of Jesus, the Incarnate and Resurrected Son of God. In recent times, this binding factor has been gradually eroded. As a result, an ordered existence of shared beliefs and values has been replaced by a chaos of conflicting ideas and individualised values. People's confidence and morale has been undermined. They no longer know what they are a part of, nor what it is that, together, they can look up to or celebrate. In a place of a shared devotion and shared values we have divisiveness and individualism.

What has been lost cannot itself be recovered. But a new binding factor can emerge through a revival of evangelism that demonstrates that continuing loving activity of the contemporary Jesus fulfilling the mission of the historic Jesus.

Jesus said, 'I, if I be lifted up, will draw all people to myself.'

Through his words, deeds, personality and authority, many of his contemporaries were attracted to him. As our contemporaries see the spiritually dead being given new life, the sick in mind, body, emotions and spirit being healed, and all who are in any kind of need being given care, hope and freedom, they too will come to see Jesus as their saviour and Lord. As their numbers grow, they will experience his friendship and will receive meaning, purpose and a shared set of values for their lives. Once again, order may grow out of chaos as we return to the path that leads to God. In the Creation, God brought order out of material chaos; in the Recreation, he will also bring order out of the new spiritual chaos.

Chapter Six

Consequences

The process of 'being transformed' has been expressed as a 'change of heart and mind'. If there is to be an understanding of what that means in practice, there needs to be an unpacking of that phrase. The first point to be made is that it is usually a gradual change that continues throughout life rather than something that happens suddenly. A change of heart involves several things – a change of feelings, a change of interests, a change of sympathies, a change of motivation, a change of likes, dislikes, attitudes and values.

A change of mind is more about how we perceive and think about things; this depends very much on early cultural conditioning and our basic assumptions and beliefs. Of course, heart and mind are not entirely separable; the emotional side of us depends to some extent, on the way we think; and the way we perceive things can depend on our feelings. So the change of heart and mind is a complex mixture of changes within someone as he or she grows in a relationship under the influence of the Holy Spirit and it has a profound effect not only on the character of a person but also on all aspects of active life. If what we are changes, what we do inevitably changes as well.

Transformed Thinking

The changes involved in being transformed as a Christian are not slight or even moderate modifications of the old creature. An entirely new creature is being born so the consequences are radical. So radical, in fact, that the whole aim and purpose of a person's life is fundamentally and irreversibly altered.

In order to appreciate the degree of change involved, it is necessary to be specific about some common things that secular society considers valuable. If a comparison is made between a brief description of how something is generally perceived in modern European society with a description that would more closely correspond to the way that it is understood in the light of Christianity, it should be possible to gain some impression of the magnitude of the difference.

Satisfaction

Personal satisfaction is something that is dear to everyone. The common view is that the greatest satisfaction is to be gained through material possessions. The more we have the better. Hence the pressure to consume conspicuously and out-do the Joneses. A Christian view is that finding out and doing what pleases God is the source of genuine personal satisfaction, even if the doing of it proves to be costly. As for material possessions, it is important for everyone to have enough to meet their everyday needs; but to have more than enough is a hindrance rather than a help.

Money

In recent years in Western Society people have become increasingly dependent on money as they do less for themselves. Instead of baking our own bread, we buy it from a baker or supermarket. It has also become more important for many people as they borrow money and become indebted. For some people who trade in currency it has gained a new and more important value because wealth can be acquired (or lost) merely by speculating on money as a commodity whose price varies.

In modern society money has become a dominant force and has acquired some of the characteristics of a religion, so that people are judged by their wealth rather than their godliness. Christianity, on the other hand, sees the worship and love of God as the overriding priority in all aspects of life. Christ is the Lord of all life and, as Jesus said, 'You cannot love God and money', for the love of money is the 'root of all evil'. Of course, this does not mean that money itself is despised by Christians. It is valued as a gift from God that is a useful means of exchange and a temporary store of value. As a servant, it is valuable; but as the master that it has become, it is a disastrous destroyer of people and communities.

The combination of the importance attached to the accumulation of material possessions and the dominant role of money is a very powerful influence on everyone born into an advanced industrial country. The change of heart and mind required to break the grip of that inherited force and to replace it with Christian perceptions and priorities is very great indeed. It is not an easy transformation to achieve in the protected environment of a monastery, so we should not be surprised at occasional falls from grace on the part of Christians who are living and working in the thick of a money-acquisitive society. Only by God's grace are we prevented from falling into that kind of temptation as we pray to be delivered from the evil of mammon-worship.

Relationships

Personal satisfaction and the role of money in everyday life are important examples of what is involved in changes of heart and mind that occur with Christian growth in consumer society. Changes just as great are involved in perceptions of behaviour in family life, marriage and sexual relationships, education, nature and life in the local and global communities. The most striking distinction between a secular view of family life, marriage, sexual relations and education and a Christian view is that the former regards individual gratification as being of supreme importance whilst Christianity recognises that people are created to live in families and communities and not merely as individuals.

Consequently, what is best for family and community is of greater importance – particularly for children or for weaker and more vulnerable members – than for any adult individual's personal gratification. The tragic consequences of a departure from a Christian view of these things are already heartbreaking and becoming steadily more destructive of people and society. Without restoration of the view that the common good transcends the individual benefit – because we are made for God and for each other – these destructive forces will hold sway. They will not only dehumanise people and communities, but education will be corrupted and nature will continue to be raped and pillaged for private gain. Privatisation in economic life is a fairly recent phenomenon, privatisation in families and communities in the form of individualisation, has a history of two centuries or more, since the Enlightenment.

Before a person becomes a Christian, attitudes and outlook are determined by the views of secular society with its emphasis on individual gratification. The process of transformation requires the replacement of those strong ideas and motivations by Christian attitudes and outlook. It is a process that has to be energised by prayer and the New Testament under the influence of the Holy Spirit, and made effective by the conscious determined effort of the person committed to please God.

Because Christians attach greater importance to the common good than to individual gratification, their response to the tensions that exist in most human relations is radically different from the responses of many non-Christians. Many of the tensions are a result of the sin of self- centredness. In the case of the non-Christian, if, as often happens, a compromise cannot be achieved, the tendency is to break the relationship; and even if a compromise is reached, nobody is entirely satisfied. Self-giving and caring for one another are the things that make the big difference for Christians when tensions are squarely faced in that spirit. When the principal aim is common good, there is no sense of second best for anyone when an agreement is reached. Instead of the relationship being either unsatisfactorily patched up or broken it is reinforced through the activity of self giving God-given Christian love. It is through self giving that the sins of self-centredness, which are the cause of tensions, are defeated. This does not mean that all is sweetness and light in Christian relationships. Christians are sinners like everyone else and suffer from all the consequences of self-centredness. The difference is that they are able to recognise the causes of tensions and seek God's forgiveness and help in overcoming them for the common good. Secular society attaches the highest value to independence. Christianity places interdependence higher.

Work

Attitudes to work is another area where a difference between a Christian and a non-Christian outlook can be seen very clearly in industrialised countries. Common secular attitudes are very confused. On the one hand, most people experience the lack of a job as a very great deprivation; but many who are employed appear to regard their work in a very negative way, despite the fact that they sometimes admit that they really quite like their work. These feelings seem to suggest that many people can see little real value or purpose in their work, other than as a necessary source of income. The fragmentised nature of many tasks that many people are undertaking day by day no doubt contributes to a sense of worthlessness. The tasks are fragmented because no importance is given to the human content of work. Workers are treated as mere factors of production.

By contrast, a Christian perception of work, whether in the form of a paid job or unpaid for one's family or others, is very positive and purposeful. The image of Jesus as the one who was involved in the creation of the universe, and in his earthly life continued in the ongoing work of creation as a carpenter, gives divine purpose to all human work. No matter how dull, repetitive and boring a task may be, it is part of universal creation. It is one of the great privileges given by God to mankind to be participants in his work. In everything that we do in every kind of work, we serve God and the rest of creation and to be fully human we need to be able to work. Nevertheless, work is not seen by Christians as the whole of life. Leisure is also important and a day of rest is ordained for that purpose. There needs to be a healthy balance.

Another important aspect of a Christian view of work is that no one kind of work is more important than another. All kinds are of equal value. Men and women have been given a variety of gifts in the form of potential abilities and skills; it is a responsibility for each person, depending on the circumstances, to make the best use possible of those gifts for the glory of God. This equal value of all kinds of work contrasts strongly with the secular hierarchical view, particularly in organisations. In a Christian view, a manager is the servant of the people for whom he or she is responsible. In the secular perception, the manager is the boss.

Linked to the concept of servant leader or manager is the concept of Christian stewardship as it applies to the use of resources involved in work, and to the view that ownership is never absolute. Many of present day environmental problems are a direct result of those perceptions and attitudes having been lost in the unconstrained, money driven industrial world.

Thankfully, there is at last a growing consensus that we have all to live within limits, treating the environment and resources with care if we are to look forward to a sustainable future. This lesson is a good illustration of the fact that a Christian outlook is universal in its application and is not something for Christians only. God's will must be done by everyone 'on earth as it is in heaven' for there is no visible alternative.

Competition

Competition now plays a bigger part than ever in all aspects of life in modern industrial countries. Unfortunately, it often has very damaging effects when it takes the form of winners and losers. The damage is sometimes so serious that it is an affront to a sense of natural justice. It causes some people to assume that all competition must be intrinsically bad whereas co-operation alone is to be fostered. Mutuality and co-operation rate high as Christian values; but competition, in the form of striving for excellence without hurt, is also viewed as pleasing to God, when its intention is for the glory of God and not personal aggrandisement.

Unhealthy competitive spirit is to be found in all parts of society, including the churches. Unfortunately, in many businesses it is looked upon as a virtue and is consequently fostered, very often with counterproductive, divisive and destructive results. It is sobering to note that, since 1986, two-thirds of the top American corporations are no longer in existence. Researchers report that most of the companies that survive are those with a strong moral code which compete by striving for excellence in all parts of their organisation.

Transformed Behaviour

Real changes of heart and mind inevitably lead to changed behaviour. It is rightly expected of every Christian that, in personal relationships in particular, there will be evidence of a neighbourly love and an absence of misbehaviours of all kinds, and most Christians are not surprised if they are so judged. However, it is less common for them to consider that there should be behavioural changes in aspects of life other than at the level of personal relationships. Indeed, some Christians consider that, to a considerable extent, they cannot be expected to depart from the common secular norms. For example, some feel that it is not possible to apply their faith in the rough and tumble of business life even though they wish that they could.

My personal experience is that, to some extent, the new outlook that develops as Christian life progresses can and does have an impact that goes well beyond matters of personal relationships. I should like to share some significant examples of the way in which my outlook and behaviour changed during my working life as an engineer, a businessman and a social innovator.

One of the most important revelations came very early during my apprenticeship. My boyhood enthusiasm was with machines. In choosing engineering as my career, my main motivation was to be immersed in the design, manufacture and operation of machines. I was particularly excited by the prospect of making them more powerful, more efficient and more automatic in operation. People were only a factor in the sense that it would be very pleasant to spend my working life with other folk who shared my interests and enthusiasms. My Christian faith was not a consideration in the choice of my engineering career; at that stage, I could see no connection.

My outlook on engineering first began to change one day when, as an apprentice, I asked the man that I was working with how he managed to maintain an intense concentration when the routine task that he was performing throughout the day, month after month, was so tedious. He was testing the hardness of aero-engine gear wheels that had been heat treated. His answer, spoken quietly and simply was, 'If I make a mistake on one of these gears, it may cost a pilot his life.'

For the first time in my life I realised that engineering is, first and foremost, concerned with people, and machines were merely their servants on which they depended. That lesson has stuck with me and had developed throughout my life, because, if engineering is really about serving the needs of people, then I must give priority to their particular requirements and, above all, must serve God's purpose for them. This remark acted as a trigger, shifting the focus of my understanding of engineering and machines – a real change of heart and mind. No longer was engineering only about fascinating machines that could perform all kinds of wonderful tricks; it was part of God's ongoing act of creation in which engineers are privileged to play a part. My colleague was simply saying that the pilot's safety depended upon the reliability of every part in his aircraft, but another voice put a different interpretation on his remark which gradually changed my whole outlook on my work.

That occurrence was the first of many more revelations that happened throughout my engineering career and beyond. From my Fleet Air Arm service as an engineer officer, I recall two more examples. In maintaining and repairing some types of aircraft, it became clear that the designers had mainly paid attention to the performance of the plane in flight and insufficient thought to the problems of keeping it in first class condition. They had made it pilot-friendly, but had forgotten that it needed also to be friendly to the people who looked after it on the ground.

This issue of relationship between the machine and the people that used it was further illustrated by the second example. For a time I had the responsibility of managing the planned programme of aircraft use and maintenance in a training squadron. The aim was to achieve the optimum use of the aircraft during a period of, say, one month. The chief flying instructor would have liked to take off in all the squadron's aircraft, whenever there were suitable conditions. Unfortunately, I could not release some aircraft on those occasions because to have done so would have upset the mandatory maintenance schedules and sub-optimised the month's overall training effort.

Naturally the chief instructor was not pleased when some serviceable aircraft were withheld when there was good flying weather. This experience told me that a machine is by no means always an obedient servant of man. The relationship is two way and operates within strict limits. If there is to be harmony, each must respect the needs of the other. But there is a fundamental difference between the needs of man and machine. Whereas those of man can be flexible, those of the machine are rigidly embodied in its design. The needs of the user have to be sympathetically considered during the design stage because once the design in set in metal there is no scope for compromise. Consequently, in the operation of a machine, all the give must come from the user, recognising the inbuilt limitations of the machine.

The lesson learned from these two experiences, or even revelations, is that the relationship between mankind and machines is not different from the relationship between mankind and nature; in both cases it is within strict limits. If we do not treat nature or machines with understanding and sympathy they will not tolerate our abuse. They will meet our needs providing we respect theirs. Nature's inflexibility is, like that of a machine, determined by its design. This being the case, if I am as an engineer involved in the design and development of machines I shall be wise to be aware of the way in which nature has been designed and operates because machines sometimes need to operate in harmony with nature.

Sometime later when I was working in the oil industry I was involved with sulphur dioxide atmospheric pollution that occurs when oil, which contains a small percentage of sulphur, is burned. A great deal of effort and money was spent in developing and building a process plant to extract sulphur from the oil. During a visit to a refinery fence in Bombay, where I had seen a splendid new processing plant, as I looked over the refinery I saw a great many very poor men, women and children. Suddenly I was struck by a thought, or revelation, that this superb engineering could be of no possible value in meeting the needs of those poor people.

This was the beginning of a new train of questioning about the kind of engineering that was being done and, indeed, about the whole process of economic development. Over the next few years, ideas such as 'appropriate technology' and 'sustainable development', which are now commonplace, began to evolve in my thinking. The process of changing heart and mind about engineering continued in me.

At a time when my interest and concern about Christian teaching about stewardship was being highlighted, part of that questioning was about the use of God given natural resources. Much of my work was concerned with the use of oil for the generation of power in all kinds of engines and for all applications. I was particularly enthusiastic to match the design of engines with the properties of fuel in order to achieve the highest possible conversion of energy. Tremendous efforts are now made to do this but, at the time, 35% efficiency was about the best that could be achieved.

One day, I was struck by the thought, or revelation, that we spent all this effort in gaining a slight improvement in efficiency, but paid almost no attention at all to the huge quantity of energy that was being thrown away in exhaust gases. When that notion was linked to the thought that I, as an engineer, needed to be aware of the processes of God's engineering in nature, I could see that our approach to power generation engineering is fundamentally flawed.

In natural processes there is no net waste; all the output is re-used as raw material for further uses within the system. The whole system is self-regulated and self-sustaining, driven only by solar energy. The kind of engineering that has been developed since the Industrial Revolution follows a linear path, unlike the closed circle path of nature. Raw materials are extracted from the earth for conversion in processes that derive their energy from limited unrenewable resources of coal, gas, oil or natural gas, and now uranium; and the products and the waste generated in their production accumulate as mountains of waste.

This kind of engineering, in the long run, is unsustainable because it depends on non renewable sources of materials and energy and is not self-sustaining because it follows a linear path that accumulates waste. To be good stewards of nature we are required to develop a new kind of engineering that recognises the waste from one process as the feed material for other processes and is dependant mainly on renewable energy sources and renewable or recyclable materials. It will be a circular engineering system – like God's engineering – rather than a linear one. In recent years this concept has begun to find some favour in expressions such as 'equilibrium engineering', 'clean technologies', 'industrial ecology' and 'sustainable development'.

Similar flashes of new insights occurred from time to time in matters of management. My initial ideas about management were no different from other people's of my generation, They were the kind of ideas that had existed for a very long time. Managers were there to give orders to a hierarchy of subordinates. It was a military command model of management, in which subordinates were expected to obey without question and certainly they were not required to think. For several years as a junior manager I had no thought of questioning whether that model was at variance with a Christian perception of management. Then something happened that startled me.

I was in Sri Lanka attending a senior managers' meeting as a technical advisor. During one session the Chairman asked each of the managers in turn to describe the essential purpose of their own company's business. I was not expecting to be asked, so I was unprepared and taken by surprise when the Chairman turned to me and asked for my response. Without hesitation, I said something like, 'it seems to me that it is a mistake to think of maximising profit as the purpose of any business' – which was, in effect, what the others present had, in different ways, been saying. 'Profit is an essential condition of survival, as eating or breathing is to life, but it cannot be the purpose. Surely our purpose must be to serve the public as best we can.' When I finished I was quite shocked at my presumption and quite prepared to be spoken to by the Chairman after the meeting, but it did not happen.

This strange and surprising incident proved to be a turning point in my career as a manager. The simple idea of service took hold and I was reminded of the image of Jesus as the Servant King. To really follow him meant that in every part of my life – even as a manager – my mission was to serve, and not only our customers, but also everyone that I managed and all with whom I worked. Working out what that meant in practice was another gradual process. Many years later, when I had retired from business, I was asked to describe in a lecture what being a servant manager meant to me. It seemed to consist of three things:

1) Working with love, which is manifested by sowing seeds of trust where suspicion and distrust exist, co-operating and promoting co-operation where acquiescence, non-co-operation and antagonism exist, and self-giving with joy and enthusiasm where self-seeking and self-advancement prevail.

2) Challenging false values which appear to be at variance with Christian values.

3) Working constructively for a better future of justice and peace

within the company and amongst the people we serve.

Finding ways of enabling the people for whom I was responsible to make the best contribution from their personal talents was an important aspect of being a servant manager. I came to realise that this can be much more difficult in a big organisation than in a small one where jobs are, to a considerable extent, fragmented. How to function in smaller scale units became a central concern in the latter years of my management career. In the last three years, I was very fortunate to have an opportunity of putting the lessons learned about the potential benefits of small-human-scale into practice in several small subsidiary companies. That practical experience confirmed my beliefs. It later proved invaluable when I became involved, after I had left the oil industry, in developing Local Enterprise Trusts, whose purpose was to assist the growth of small firms. The assistance given is provided by established companies voluntarily joining together for the wellbeing of the local economy in a spirit of community.

Sixteen years after that first flash of insight in the Bombay Refinery, my whole outlook had changed with respect to both engineering and economic development. Thereafter, I had to search for practical ways, and with a new heart and mind, to help people live dignified lives in harmony with nature and in peace with each other, both in Bombay and Birmingham. The whole aim and purpose of my working life had been fundamentally changed.

Someone else said about me that, 'in his fifties (he) entered his age of renewal, searching into parts of himself that had lain dormant for so many years. More recently, (he) has taken the further step of integrating the two parts of himself.'

I believe the person was describing the process and the consequences of being transformed as it occurred to me in my own working life, as I have explained. Other Christians will have their own stories to tell of being transformed because they too will have responded to the call of St Paul to the Romans (Chapter 12, verses 1-2), 'Don't let the world around you squeeze you into its own mould, but let God remake you so that your whole attitude of mind and your whole nature is transformed. Then you will be able to discern the will of God and to know what is good, acceptable and perfect.'

No doubt, Paul knew that it was God alone who had remade and transformed his whole nature and attitude of mind. If he had followed his old natural inclinations, he would have continued to be a militant Jew and to persecute Christians. Paul recognised, as I have, that God fulfils the promise he gave to the prophet Ezekiel (Chapter 36, verses 26-27), 'I will give you a new heart and a new mind ... I will put my spirit into you so that you may conform to my ways and live by them.'

I know for certain that it was God that brought about the transformation in me, despite all my waywardness, because, if I had gone my own way, I should have followed a very different path. Thank God that, when I was a young man, he chose to begin to remake me. Over fifty years later, I am still far from being fully transformed. Despite my obduracy, God remains faithful to his Ezekiel promise; his patience is unlimited.

As well as transformed thinking and behaviour, there are valuable other benefits that come as consequences of living the life of a Christian. Like changes in thinking and behaviour, these benefits don't all come suddenly when you first become a follower of Jesus; they come gradually as your relationship with him develops from experience and prayer.

These benefits are a wonderful gift and are personally very rewarding. They are beautifully described by Paul in the fifth chapter of his letter to the Christians in Galatia. Having reminded his readers in a list of the horrible things that are done as a result of human self-centredness, he tells them of the freedom from them which they can experience if their lives are guided by the Holy Spirit within them. From his own experience since he became a Christian, he describes these qualities as, 'fruits of the Spirit – love joy, peace, patience, gentleness, goodness, faith, meekness and temperance'. Where they do not exist naturally in a person's make-up, experience tells us that they are almost impossible to develop, even with a considerable effort, without the help and guidance gained through daily prayer to be free from temptation with an ability to discern anything evil.

Freedom from the things we most dislike about ourselves and the gift of the qualities which we most admire is truly a great benefit.

In the Introduction to this book it was stated that one aim was to throw some light on such questions as, 'What does it mean to be a Christian?' and, 'Does it make any difference to the way that a person lives now?' and, if so, 'What difference does it make?' The ordinary life illustrations of transformed thinking, transformed behaviour and the wonderful gift of changed character, described as, 'fruits of the Spirit', make clear that by taking Jesus seriously, by putting complete trust in him, the potential benefits to life here and now are so great as to be almost beyond description. They amount to nothing less than an entirely new life with God.

This is exactly what Jesus promised to his faithful followers who were prepared to give up everything for him. This new life is full of the things we most admire and desire for ourselves and everyone else. There is nothing on earth to equal it and the proof of the pudding is in the eating.

The wonderful thing about Christianity is that it is a relationship, the very best kind of relationship, where both give all to each other.

St Aidan brought Christianity to northern England in the seventh century. He expressed it perfectly in a prayer;

Lord
You give me life
You give me love
You give me joy
You give me peace
You give me yourself
In you I am enriched

Help me to share
To give what I receive
Help me to give my life
To give my love
To give myself
In the service of others
And to you, Giver of all.

From all that Jesus did and does and teaches, we can give added meaning to that beautiful prayer;

Lord
You give me life – life with you, a new and changed life
You give me love – because you, the source of love, live in me
You give me joy – through freedom from self-centredness
You give me peace – through confidence and freedom from
anxiety and fear
You give me yourself – to guide me and make choices that please
you
In you I am enriched – beyond all that I can imagine
Help me to share – freely all of the talents you have given me
To give what I receive – from you, all that will further your purpose
Help me to give my life – to your purposes for me, and not to my
ambition
To give my love – to those people and things I find unlovable
To give myself - to care for your creation
In the service of others
And to you, Giver of all.

As we have seen from the consequences of a life of trust in Jesus, the Christian life can be one of lovely surprises and an exciting adventure.

Chapter Seven

Beliefs – Christianity and Churchianity

In Chapter 2 various common misconceptions of what Christianity is were described. One misunderstanding is that assent to a set of beliefs is its essence, whereas, in reality it is a relationship with the living and active Jesus. However, that relationship necessarily involves a conviction that there was a man called Jesus of Nazareth some two thousand years ago who is still alive and active.

All kinds of people all over the world – by no means only Christians – believe that the man called Jesus, who is the central character in the New Testament, lived in Palestine two thousand years ago. That belief is the same kind of belief, which is supported by independent contemporary historical records, as in a King called Henry VIII.

But belief in Jesus who is still alive and active is a very different kind of belief. We cannot rely solely on the statements of his disciples who claimed to see him after his crucifixion, simply because they are not alive today to be able to confirm that he is still alive and active at the present time. That belief is only credible if there are people living today who claim to experience him and his activity. But it is such an extraordinary claim that it cannot be absolutely convincing unless it is personally experienced.

During World War II, I read about Douglas Bader, the legless fighter pilot. When I joined Shell, a colleague who had met him told me about some of his exploits before the War in Shell's London office.

Then one day I met him at work and he became a reality to me. At each stage there was a different kind of belief – reading about him, being told about him by someone who knew him, and then becoming acquainted with him myself. There are the same three stages of belief about Jesus – reading about the historic and risen Jesus as described by his contemporaries, learning from people at present who claim to have direct experience of him, and finally sharing in that experience, which makes all the difference.

Trust comes from experience. The longer the experience lasts, providing the experience is consistent, trust grows. It can only be destroyed when experience proves it to be false. Christian belief in Jesus means to have total trust in him. As he says to his disciples (John, Chapter 14), 'Trust always in God and also trust me.'

Core Christian beliefs are all of this kind. They are trust based on personal experience. They are not merely intellectual or emotional assents to an historical record or a set of dogmatic statements. That is why all the arguments about the truth of the Bible stories about Jesus are so futile. You may be able to find reasons and evidence that convinced me that what I had read or been told about Douglas Bader were not strictly true, but that would not cause me to doubt his existence once I had met him and got to know him.

There are two categories of belief amongst Christians. There are what might be described as 'core beliefs' which are shared by Christians of all denominations. Then there are other beliefs about which there is a good deal of disagreement. The 'core beliefs' do not depend on the authority of the Bible or any particular historical tradition or individual. They are of the kind described in the previous paragraphs, having their authority based on the common experience of people today and in times past. Just as it is possible for anyone to confirm for themselves that the force of gravity exists by observing, as Isaac Newton did, an apple falling from a tree, it is equally possible for a person to discover for themselves the truth of the core Christian beliefs through an experiment of prayer that the truth of the 'core-belief' is learned. Because the experiment of prayer is repeated time and time again, assurance develops which cannot be shaken.

It is interesting to note that confidence in core Christian beliefs has the same basis as confidence in the findings of scientists. I recall that when I was a young research engineer, a particular type of aero-engine had sparking plugs that failed for no obvious reason. A colleague guessed that an electric short was occurring on the surface of the sparking plug insulator because there was a very thin, invisible deposit which was acting as a conductor. The only way to prove whether this theory was right or wrong was to conduct an experiment.

A little something was added to the fuel that we knew for certain would increase the electrical resistance of any deposit that might be formed on the sparking plug insulator and there were no more failures. The experiment was repeated many times under different conditions until we were completely convinced that the theory was correct. Whenever we removed what we had added, it changed the electrical resistance of the deposits and the engine failed. In the life of a Christian, prayer is the addition that makes all the difference. We know that it is true because we have tried it many, many times.

Although Christians and all kinds of scientists validate their beliefs experimentally and by experience, they are describing quite different

81

categories of experience. Scientists are concerned with obtaining as clear a picture of the workings of nature as they possibly can. Christians are concerned with obtaining as clear a picture as possible of God and his purposes for his creation. Of course, Christians, who are also scientists – and happily there are many – are concerned with both searches for truth. What scientists discover may, or may not, lead to action; what Christians learn must lead to action, because prayer inevitably changes people and people change things as a result. If you discover what you believe to be God's will in a particular situation, you must act upon it as your desire is to please God.

With the understanding that Christian 'core beliefs' are validated by centuries of experience of millions of Christians all over the world, we can now give the results of all that experience. We must begin at the beginning – or even before the beginning – with God. Since the earliest times of human history there has been a deep seated notion of the existence of god-like beings that were ascribed many different characteristics by different peoples. The one God that Christians know and experience partially is invisible and beyond time and space. Nevertheless, he is accessible and communication can take place at a spiritual level. All experience reveals that he is the Creator and Sustainer of the universe, for which he has unlimited love and care, who desires a close and co-operative relationship with all people, but without any compulsion – a mutual relationship of love.

The second core-belief concerns ourselves. The more we become aware of the nature and character of God – particularly his self giving love and care for all his creation, the more we can see our own self-centredness, which is the thing that interferes with our relationship with

God. It appears to be inherent in our nature. Perhaps that is what is meant by the term original sin. Not all are equally self centred, but it is present to varying degrees in everyone. It manifests itself in many different ways. Every one of the seven deadly sins appear to have their roots in self-centredness; pride, covetousness, lust, anger, gluttony, envy, sloth. It is a very destructive condition, not only of our relationship with God, but also of our relationships with one another. It seems to be at the root of all the trouble in the world. The more we try, the more we come to recognise that we cannot from our own resources alone escape from its grip. St Paul admitted that it was a human impossibility to master ungodly instincts without the spiritual help that could come only from God.

The third core-belief is that, as Jesus said, 'God so loved the world that he gave his only begotten son,' to meet that very need of conquering the sin that imprisons us all. Jesus, who was both God and man, during his short life on earth, gave us the clearest picture that human understanding can comprehend of what God is like. It was his perfect Godliness that led to his crucifixion.

And our fourth core-belief is that in his Resurrection he overcame physical death and continues to this day to live and be active in the world. This is the great certainty, because we get to know him better day by day. It also happens to be the absolute assurance of life in a New Creation that exists here and now as well as beyond time and space. Although St Paul never met Jesus during his lifetime, he, probably more than any of the disciples, was conscious of the indwelling and constant presence of the Risen Jesus in his life. He stated, 'For me to live is Christ, to die is gain.' It is something echoed by all the saints in every age.

The final core-belief is that the free and undeserved gift of God's Holy Spirit is available to be claimed by anyone, no matter how unworthy, who longs to be transformed from their self-centredness into the person God wants them to be.

Every one of these five core beliefs is personally testified on the basis of experience, as well as by scripture and the institutional Churches. They are entirely trustworthy and not capable of contradiction. They are all embodied in historic creeds.

But there is more in the historic creeds than those core-beliefs alone, and many more beliefs are associated with the various denominational churches. All of these lack the essential element of personal experience and are entirely based on the interpretations of scripture and the different historic tradition of parts of the worldwide Christian communion. Sadly, it is some of these non core beliefs which have been, and still are, in some places, the source of division and antagonism between adherents of different interpretations. Although it seems self evident that no simple interpretation can be said to be not capable of contradiction, some of these beliefs are held by individual Christians as absolute truth and as essential to faith as the core beliefs themselves. Thus, when someone says that they do not believe in the Virgin Birth of our Lord as a matter of historic fact, they are considered by some to be as guilty of heresy as if they said they do not believe Jesus is alive and active.

The core-beliefs, which are common to all Christians and are the foundation of faith, can be said to be the essence of Christianity from which energy and loving self-sacrifice is generated. Some of the many non-core-beliefs, which can be described as Churchianity, because of their divisiveness, seriously detract from the power of the faith to transform human life. The more that non-core-beliefs can be perceived as fallible interpretations rather than as representing absolute truth, the more can God's will be done.

The development of non-core-beliefs by groups of non-Christians began during the lives of the apostles, as is clear from the Epistles. It has continued ever since with an inevitable fragmentation of believers into many different forms of institutionalised religion. During the early centuries there were various attempts to condemn some beliefs as heresies and to formulate creeds. These contained statements agreed between the various leaders of various sections of the Christian Churches, laying down a number of common beliefs. They were very much like political communiqués, setting out what was agreed at an important meeting.

The Creeds for those early centuries have remained as the official statements of belief of all Church denominations which bind them together. Whilst they do refer to the core-belief of all Christianity, in certain respects they do so inadequately. For example, The Nicene Creed mentions one God, the Father and Creator, but says nothing about the kind of God that he is (eg: a God of Love). Consequently, even today, some sincere practising Christians perceive God as an Old Testament, punishing God. Even worse, some prayers in the Anglican Prayer Book tend to confirm that image. One of the statements of beliefs, which is not at all a core-belief, concerns the Virgin Birth of Jesus. This is still a source of much dissension and many devoted followers of Jesus reject it. So even these historic credal statements divide as well as bind Christians together, as well as being incomplete, particularly about the character of God.

Over the centuries, many more non-core-beliefs have been added by both the Western (Roman) and the Eastern (Greek and Russian) Churches. As a result, for example, a modern Roman Catholic is required to assent to some beliefs demanded by Popes in the last two hundred years which were not previously considered to be essential to salvation and which certainly did not come from Jesus. At the Reformation, many more statements of belief began to be formulated which led to a fragmentation of the non-conformist denominations. The Thirty Nine Articles of Faith of the Anglican Communion is one example, to which all Priests must publicly assent at the preparation for their ordination. This statement, produced at the time of the first Queen Elizabeth, is strongly coloured by the religious conflicts of the time which no longer exist. Even the doctrine of the Virgin Birth and the Bodily Resurrection almost provided a stumbling block to William Temple at this first approach to ordination.

Not only have the non-core-beliefs divided the Church of Christ into many scandalous denominations, even within a Church, such as the Methodist, Baptist and Anglican, but also there are internal divisions based on different emphases of the importance of particular aspects of their body of belief. These are sometimes the cause of great and destructive tensions between members. Many of the main disagreements between denominations concern the source of authority within the institution and nature of ministers. Some are so deep that one Church rejects the validity of the others, for example, whether ministers are in an unbroken line of the Apostolic Succession. Other disagreements which run deep concern the Sacraments of Baptism and

Holy Communion. Other divisions have developed over the past century on matters of Christian marriage and divorce, despite the clear teaching of Jesus on these matters.

In the long history of Christianity there have been continuing disagreements about the Scriptures, and the role of reason in their interpretation. Even to the present day, there are many fundamentalists who insist on a literal meaning for every passage and refuse to acknowledge the findings of modern scholarship. It was from a rigid unwillingness of Christian leaders and scholars in the 19th century to recognise the possibility of an evolutionary process of creation that has been an important cause of the secularisation which has since occurred in most of the Christian world. The Churches lost credibility.

None of these issues, which so divide and weaken Christianity, is concerned with its essence, which is a way of life lived in total trust and devotion to Jesus and inspired by the Holy Spirit. By creating a divided institutional religion bearing the name of Christ, Jesus has been betrayed. It was the hierarchy of Judaism, which he criticised for their elevation of minute legalism, and their indifference to love, justice, compassion and forgiveness, that were his enemy. By constructing ever more elaborate structures of belief, religious rituals and organisations, Churchianity has fallen into the trap of adopting many of the characteristics which Jesus opposed in the religion of his day. There can be little doubt that the dominant view within Christianity of what most distinguishes a devoted Christian is regular attendance in congregational worship. There can also be little doubt that such practice would have little value for Jesus unless it was a small part of lives lived unselfishly and sacrificially with love for fellow human beings and with care for God's Creation.

Before he was ordained, in a letter to his friend, John L Stocks, William Temple, who later became Archbishop of Canterbury, wrote the following astonishing sentences;

'What is our so-called Christianity doing? Men are still encouraged to get drunk than otherwise; the poor are not housed, nor the naked clothed, nor the hungry fed. And yet nearly everyone in England professes to believe that at least one of the sentences of final condemnation (by Jesus) is, 'I was a stranger and ye took me not in etc'. Take another instance: it is a certain fact that, in rich parishes, the people who go to Church are the most selfish. And yet our Lord said, 'Not everyone that saith unto me 'Lord, Lord', shall enter into the kingdom of heaven; but he that doeth the will of my Father' - i.e. his duty to his neighbour. I might give instances for ever: but to put it shortly, the Church forgets that Christianity is not just an attitude of mind, but a type of life: a man's spirit is known not by his opinion (creeds etc) but by his actions and general conduct. Well, I believe the only thing that can save us (the Church) is a vigorous attack from within the Church on the existing conceptions of religion. In short, anything more hostile to the New Testament than our modern English religion is hard to conceive.'

Sadly, a century later, nothing much has changed. Nevertheless, despite the differences of understanding and interpretation of the Christian faith amongst the institutions, they still represent a family home for individual Christians, where they can share fellowship and support one another in their journey of discipleship of Jesus. Also, and importantly, they can gather together week by week to renew their commitment to Jesus and to accept his invitation, made at the Last Supper, to take and eat bread and to drink wine in remembrance of him, giving thanks for the forgiveness and new life that he has made possible for the world. It is through this common act of worship that the unity of Christianity can be expressed. It cannot be divided, no matter what differences may exist between the institutions. We must not allow those differences to distract us from a commitment to Jesus.